POCKET

EDINBURGH

TOP SIGHTS · LOCAL EXPERIENCES

D0963956

NEIL WILSON

Contents

Plan Your Trip

Exterior of the Scottish Parliament Building (p74)
CORNFIELD/SHUTTERSTOCK ©

Explore Edinburgh   33

Worth a Trip

Survival Guide   161

Special Features

Welcome to Edinburgh

Edinburgh is one of Britain's most beautiful and dramatic cities, with its castle perched on the summit of ancient crags and the medieval maze of the Old Town gazing across verdant gardens to the elegant Georgian squares and streetscapes of the New Town. History and architecture are leavened with vibrant bars, innovative restaurants and Scotland's most stylish shops.

Cityscape view from Calton Hill (p97)

VICHIE81/SHUTTERSTOCK ©

Top Sights

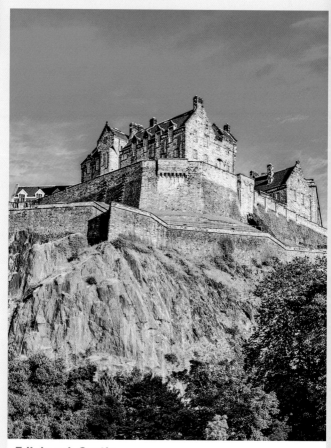

Edinburgh Castle
Scotland's most popular tourist attraction. **p36**

Real Mary King's Close

Lost world beneath the streets. **p40**

National Museum of Scotland

Treasure house of Scottish culture. **p42**

Palace of Holyroodhouse

The Queen's Edinburgh residence. **p72**

Scottish Parliament Building

Visual feast of modern architecture. **p74**

Scottish National Portrait Gallery

Visual encyclopedia of famous Scots. **p86**

Princes Street Gardens

Green oasis in the city centre. **p88**

Scottish National Gallery of Modern Art

Masterpieces of contemporary art. **p112**

Royal Botanic Garden

Tranquil haven of lush greenery. **p124**

Royal Yacht Britannia

Royal family's floating palace. **p136**

Rosslyn Chapel

Medieval mystery carved in stone. **p158**

Eating

Eating out in Edinburgh has changed beyond all recognition since the 1990s. Back then, sophisticated dining meant a visit to the Aberdeen Angus Steak House for a prawn cocktail, steak (well done) and chips, and Black Forest gateau. Today, Edinburgh has more restaurants per head of population than any other UK city, including a handful of places with Michelin stars.

Modern Scottish Cuisine

Scotland has never been celebrated for its national cuisine – in fact, from haggis and porridge to deep-fried Mars bars, it has more often been an object of ridicule. But since the early 2000s chefs have been taking top-quality Scottish produce – from Highland venison, Aberdeen Angus beef and freshly landed seafood to root vegetables, raspberries and Ayrshire cheeses – and preparing it simply, in a way that emphasises the natural flavours.

Haggis – Scotland's National Dish

The raw ingredients of Scotland's national dish don't sound too promising – the finely chopped lungs, heart and liver of a sheep, mixed with oatmeal and onion and stuffed into a sheep's stomach bag. However, it tastes surprisingly good and is on the menu in many restaurants, whether served with the traditional accompaniment of mashed potatoes and turnip, or given a modern twist such as haggis in filo pastry parcels (pictured).

Best Modern Scottish

Timberyard Seasonally changing menu sourced from artisan growers and foragers. (p115)

Aizle A set menu of the finest and freshest of local produce. (p151)

Castle Terrace Faultless cuisine from chef-patron Dominic Jack, protégé of TV's *Tom Kitchin*. (p115)

Wedgwood Foraged salad leaves add originality to informal fine dining. (p59)

Best Traditional Scottish

Tower Specialities include Scottish oysters and Aberdeen Angus steaks, and there's a great view of the castle. (p59)

KAWIN TOWE/SHUTTERSTOCK ©

Amber Set in the Scotch Whisky Experience, many dishes include whisky in the recipe. (p61)

McKirdy's Steakhouse Prime Scottish beef, simply prepared and served in a friendly, informal setting. (p116)

Witchery by the Castle Wonderfully over-the-top Gothic decor, great steak and seafood, and fine wines. (p59)

Best Seafood

Ondine Beautiful dining room, with menu based on sustainably sourced fish. (p56)

Fishers Bistro A local institution, with North Berwick lobster a speciality. (p140)

Shore Pleasantly informal restaurant with Leith waterfront setting; serves game as well as seafood. (p141)

Best Vegetarian

David Bann Smart and sophisticated, bringing an inventive approach to vegetarian food. (p60)

Kalpna Long-established Indian restaurant, famous for its all-you-can-eat lunch buffet. (p153)

Henderson's The grandmother of Edinburgh's vegetarian scene, around since 1962. (p103)

Top Tips

∘ Book well in advance (at least a month ahead for August) to be sure of a table at Edinburgh's top restaurants.

∘ The *Edinburgh & Glasgow Eating & Drinking Guide* (http://food.list.co.uk), published annually by *The List* magazine, contains reviews of several hundred restaurants, cafes and bars.

∘ The www.5pm.co.uk website lists last-minute offers from restaurants with tables to spare that evening.

Drinking

Edinburgh has always been a drinker's city. It has more than 700 pubs – more per square mile than any other UK city – and they are as varied and full of character as the people who drink in them, from Victorian palaces to stylish pre-club bars, and from real-ale howffs (meeting places, often pubs) to cool cocktail lounges.

Edinburgh Beers

By the end of the 19th century, Edinburgh ranked alongside Munich, Pilsen and Burton-on-Trent in importance as a brewing centre, with no fewer than 35 breweries. Today the city's two large-scale breweries – Caledonian (now owned by Heineken), creator of Deuchars IPA (available in most of the city's real-ale pubs); and Stewart Brewing, producer of Edinburgh Gold – have been joined by an ever-growing number of microbreweries and brewpubs.

Trad vs Trendy

At one end of Edinburgh's broad spectrum of hostelries lies the traditional 19th-century pub, which has preserved much of its original Victorian decoration and generally serves real ales and a range of malt whiskies. At the other end is the modern cocktail bar, with a cool clientele and sharp styling.

Opening Times

Pubs generally open from 11am to 11pm Monday to Saturday and 12.30pm to 11pm on Sunday. Many open later on Friday and Saturday, closing at midnight or 1am, while some with a music licence party on until 3am.

Best Historic Pubs

Bennet's Bar Locals pub with lovely Victorian fittings. (p154)

Café Royal Circle Bar City-centre haven of Victorian splendour, famed for Doulton ceramic portraits. (p103)

Sheep Heid Inn Semi-rural retreat in the shadow of Arthur's Seat, famed as Edinburgh's oldest pub. (p82)

Guildford Arms A time capsule of polished mahogany and gleaming brass. (p104)

LOU ARMOR/SHUTTERSTOCK ©

Best Real-Ale Pubs

Holyrood 9A Modern take on a trad pub, with no fewer than 20 beers on tap. (p64)

Blue Blazer Resolutely old-fashioned pub with good range of Scottish ales. (p118)

Auld Hoose Great jukebox plus broad range of beers from Scottish microbreweries. (p155)

Best Cocktail Bars

Bramble Possibly the city's best cocktails, served in an atmospheric cellar bar. (p104)

Tigerlily Cocktails as colourful as the swirling, glittering designer decor. (p107)

Lucky Liquor Co Tiny but highly rated bar serving inventive and unusual cocktails. (p104)

Best Whisky Bars

Bow Bar Busy Grassmarket-area pub with huge selection of malt whiskies. (p62)

Malt Shovel Old-school pub with more than 100 single malts behind the bar. (p64; pictured)

Last Word Saloon Small but well-chosen selection; good place to dip a toe in the world of whisky. (p131)

Top Tips

○ The **Gig Guide** (www.gigguide. co.uk) is a free monthly email newsletter and listings website covering live music in Edinburgh pubs.

○ If you want to avoid crowds on Friday and Saturday nights, steer clear of the Grassmarket, the Cowgate and Lothian Rd.

Shopping

Edinburgh's shopping experience extends far beyond the big-name department stores of Princes St, ranging from designer fashion and handmade jewellery to independent bookshops, delicatessens and farmers markets. Classic north-of-the-border buys include cashmere, Harris tweed, tartan goods, Celtic jewellery, smoked salmon and Scotch whisky.

Princes Street

Princes St is Edinburgh's trademark shopping strip, lined with big high-street names including Marks & Spencer, Debenhams and the Apple Store. There are more designer boutiques a block north on George St, and many smaller specialist stores on Rose St and Thistle St. There are also two big city-centre shopping malls – Princes Mall, at the eastern end of Princes St, and the new Edinburgh St James (scheduled to open in 2020), at the top of Leith St – plus Multrees Walk, a designer shopping complex with flagship Harvey Nichols store on the eastern side of St Andrew Sq.

Shopping Districts

Other central shopping streets include South Bridge, Nicolson St and Lothian Rd. For more offbeat shopping – including fashion, music, crafts, gifts and jewellery – head for Cockburn, Victoria and St Mary's Sts, all leading off the Royal Mile; William St in the West End; and Raeburn Pl and St Stephen's St in Stockbridge. Ocean Terminal, in Leith, is the city's biggest mall.

Best Department Stores

Jenners An Edinburgh shopping institution, stocking a wide range of quality goods, both classic and contemporary. (p93)

Harvey Nichols Four floors of designer labels and eye-popping price tags. (p93)

John Lewis Classic British store with a focus on quality goods and service. (p109)

Best for Tartan

Kinloch Anderson Tailors and kiltmakers to HM the Queen and HRH the Duke of Edinburgh; 'nuff said. (p144)

JAROSLAV MORAVCIK/SHUTTERSTOCK ©

Geoffrey (Tailor) Inc Kilts in all patterns, from clan tartans to football colours. (p68)

21st Century Kilts Fashion kilts in modern fabrics, from camouflage to leather. (p93)

Best Markets

Edinburgh Farmers Market Saturday feast of fresh Scottish produce, from smoked venison to organic free-range eggs. (p116)

Stockbridge Market Eclectic Sunday market that has become a focus for the local community. (p132)

The Pitt Weekly street-food market. (p141)

Best for Jewellery

Galerie Mirages Best known for its silver, amber and gemstone jewellery. (p133)

Alchemia Original designs as well as specially commissioned pieces. (p93)

Annie Smith Edinburgh designer famed for beautiful and delicate pieces reflecting nature's patterns. (p133)

Best for Books

Lighthouse Long-established radical bookshop specialising in political, gay and feminist literature. (p157)

McNaughtan's Bookshop Secondhand and antiquarian dealer with books on Scottish history, art and architecture. (p109)

Top Tips

○ In shops displaying a 'Tax Free' sign, visitors from non-EU countries can claim back the 20% VAT (value-added tax) they have paid on purchased goods.

○ Many city-centre shops stay open till 7pm or 8pm on Thursday.

Museums & Galleries

As Scotland's capital city, it's hardly surprising that Edinburgh is home to some of the country's most important museums and art collections. You can admire the Old Masters at the Scottish National Gallery, hone your knowledge of Scottish heritage at the National Museum of Scotland, or delve into the arcane delights of the city's lesser-known collections.

Special Events

Several of the city's major institutions host special events and after-hours visits. The National Museum of Scotland stages Museum After Hours events throughout the year, with live music, lectures and behind-the-scenes tours; while the National Gallery of Scotland and the National Portrait Gallery stage musical performances, educational talks and art lessons. Check the museum's website What's On or Events links for details.

Admission & Access

National collections (eg National Museum of Scotland, Scottish National Gallery, Scottish National Portrait Gallery, Scottish National Gallery of Modern Art) and Edinburgh city-owned museums (Museum of Edinburgh, City Art Centre etc) have free admission, except for temporary exhibitions where a fee is often charged. Most private galleries are also free; smaller museums often charge an entrance fee, typically around £5 (book online at some museums for discounted tickets). National collections are generally open from 10am to 5pm, with the Scottish National Gallery staying open till 7pm on Thursday.

Best Collections

National Museum of Scotland Beautiful setting for collections covering Scottish history, the natural world, art and engineering. (p42; pictured)

Scottish National Portrait Gallery Far more interesting than the name implies, especially after a recent revamp. (p86)

FRANCESCO RICCIARDI EXP/SHUTTERSTOCK ©

Scottish National Gallery
Old masters, Scottish artists, and Canova's famous marble sculpture of the Three Graces. (p96)

Scottish National Gallery of Modern Art Pride of place goes to works by the Scottish Colourists, Eduardo Paolozzi and Barbara Hepworth. (p112)

Best Smaller Museums

Museum of Edinburgh
The city: Stone Age to 20th century. (p52)

Surgeons' Hall Museums
Grisly but fascinating collection on the history of surgery. (p150)

Writers' Museum All you ever wanted to know about Robert Burns, Walter Scott and Robert Louis Stevenson. (p53)

Best Museum Architecture

Scottish National Portrait Gallery Gorgeous palace in Venetian Gothic style, studded with sculptures of famous Scots. (p86)

National Museum of Scotland Staid Victorian building set off by flamboyant modern extension in golden sandstone. (p42)

Museum of Edinburgh Set in a 16th-century house with colourful, ornate decoration in red and yellow ochre. (p52)

Top Tips

∘ The national collections have useful 'trail' leaflets that guide you around their highlights.

∘ All major museums and galleries have good restaurants or cafes, often worth a visit in their own right.

Festivals & Events

Edinburgh is one of the biggest party venues in the world, with a crowded calendar of contrasting festivals. High season is August, when half a dozen festivals – including the huge Edinburgh International Festival, and the even bigger Festival Fringe – run concurrently. It's closely followed by the Christmas festival in December, which runs into the Hogmanay celebrations.

Edinburgh International Festival

First held in 1947 to mark a return to peace after the ordeal of WWII, the Edinburgh International Festival is festooned with superlatives – the oldest, the biggest, the most famous, the best in the world. The festival takes place over the three weeks ending on the first Saturday in September; the program is usually available from April. Tickets sell out quickly, so it's best to book as far in advance as possible.

Edinburgh Festival Fringe

When the first Edinburgh International Festival was held in 1947, there were eight theatre companies that didn't make it onto the main program. Undeterred, they grouped together and held their own mini-festival, on the fringe, and an Edinburgh institution was born. The Fringe (pictured) takes place over 3½ weeks, the last two overlapping with the first two of the Edinburgh International Festival.

Best Festivals

Edinburgh International Science Festival (April) Hosts a wide range of events, including talks, lectures, exhibitions, demonstrations, guided tours and interactive experiments designed to stimulate, inspire and challenge.

Imaginate Festival (May) Britain's biggest festival of performing arts for children, with events suitable for kids aged three to 12 years. Groups from around the world perform classic tales like Hansel and Gretel, as well as new material written specially for children.

Edinburgh International Film Festival (June) The two-week film festival is a major international event, serving as a showcase for

JOHANN KNOX/SHUTTERSTOCK ©

new British and European films, and staging the European premieres of one or two Hollywood blockbusters.

Edinburgh International Festival (August) Hundreds of the world's top musicians and performers congregate for three weeks of diverse and inspirational music, opera, theatre and dance.

Edinburgh Festival Fringe (August) The biggest festival of the performing arts anywhere in the world.

Edinburgh Military Tattoo (August) A spectacular display of military marching bands, massed pipes and drums, acrobats, cheerleaders and motorcycle display teams, all played out in front of the magnificent backdrop of the floodlit castle.

Edinburgh International Book Festival (August)

A fun fortnight of talks, readings, debates, lectures, book signings and meet-the author events.

Best Events

Beltane (April/May) A pagan fire festival, resurrected in modern form, marking the end of winter, celebrated on the summit of Calton Hill.

Royal Highland Show (late June) A four-day feast of all

things rural, from tractor driving to sheep shearing.

Edinburgh's Christmas (December) Includes a street parade, fairground and Ferris wheel, and an open-air ice rink in Princes Street Gardens.

Edinburgh's Hogmanay (From 29 December to 1 January) Events include a torchlight procession and huge street party.

Top Tips

The comprehensive source for what's-on info is *The List* (www.list.co.uk), an excellent listings website and magazine covering both Edinburgh and Glasgow. It's available from most newsagents, and is published every two months.

Architecture

Edinburgh's beauty arises from a combination of its unusual site, perched among craggy hills, and a legacy of fine architecture dating from the 16th century to the present day. The New Town remains the world's most complete and unspoilt example of Georgian architecture and town planning. Along with the Old Town, it was declared a Unesco World Heritage Site in 1995.

Old Town Tenements

Edinburgh's Old Town features the biggest concentration of surviving 17th-century buildings in Britain. These tenements, six to eight storeys high, were among the tallest in Britain in their time. You can explore such tenements at Gladstone's Land (p53) and John Knox House (p54).

Georgian Gorgeousness

Robert Adam (1728–92), one of the leading architects of the Georgian period, made his mark in Edinburgh's New Town with neoclassical masterpieces such as Charlotte Square (p96) and Edinburgh University's Old College. Experience the elegance of Adam's interiors by visiting the Georgian House (p96).

Modern Masterpiece

The plan for the New Town was the result of a competition won by James Craig, then an unknown, self-taught 23-year-old architect. At the end of the 20th century another architectural competition resulted in the relatively unknown Enric Miralles being chosen as the architect for the new Scottish Parliament Building (p74). Though its construction was controversial, the building won the 2005 Stirling Prize for the best new architecture in Britain, and has revitalised a near-derelict industrial site at the foot of the Royal Mile.

Best Modern Architecture

Scottish Parliament Building Ambitious, controversial and way over budget: the most exciting example of modern architecture in Scotland. (p74; pictured)

CLAUDIO DIVIZIA/SHUTTERSTOCK ©

National Museum of Scotland The museum's golden sandstone lines create echoes of castles, churches, gardens and cliffs. (p42)

Scottish Poetry Library Award-winning building, cleverly insinuated into a cramped space in an Old Town alley. (p81)

Front Range The designer glasshouses in Edinburgh's Royal Botanic Garden, built in 1967, are included in *Prospect* magazine's Top 100 Modern Scottish Buildings. (p124)

Best Neoclassical Architecture

Charlotte Square The elegantly proportioned Adam facade on the square's north side is the jewel in the New Town's architectural crown. (p96)

Royal Scottish Academy This imposing William Playfair–designed Doric temple dominates the centre of Princes St. (p96)

Dundas House Gorgeous Palladian mansion that now houses a bank; pop into the main hall for a look at the dome, painted blue and studded with glazed stars. (p99)

Best Early Architecture

George Heriot's School Imposing Renaissance building (1628–1650), funded by George Heriot (nicknamed Jinglin' Geordie), goldsmith and jeweller to King James VI. (p47)

Parliament Hall Dating from 1639, this grandiose hall has a majestic hammer-beam roof, and was home to the Scottish Parliament until the 1707 Act of Union. (p56)

Best Monuments

Scott Monument This Gothic space rocket parked amid the greenery of Princes Street Gardens celebrates Scotland's most famous historical novelist, Sir Walter Scott. (p89)

Nelson Monument Built in the shape of an upturned telescope, this slender tower on the summit of Calton Hill was built to commemorate Nelson's victory at Trafalgar in 1805. (p97)

National Monument An unfinished folly atop Calton Hill; its Greek temple–like appearance gave Edinburgh the nickname 'Athens of the North'. (p98)

Views

/GETTY IMAGES ©

Edinburgh is one of Europe's most beautiful cities, draped across a series of rocky hills overlooking the sea. A glance in any souvenir shop will reveal a display of postcards that testify to the city's many viewpoints, both natural and artificial. Part of the pleasure of any visit to Edinburgh is simply soaking up the scenery, so set aside some time to explore the loftier parts of the city, camera in hand.

Best Natural Viewpoints

Arthur's Seat Sweeping panoramas from the highest point in Edinburgh. (p79)

Calton Hill Edinburgh's templed 'acropolis' affords a superb view along Princes St. (p97)

Blackford Hill This southern summit provides a grandstand view of Castle Rock and Arthur's Seat. (p151; pictured)

Best Architectural Viewpoints

Scott Monument Climb 287 steps to the top of this Gothic pinnacle, and look out over Princes Street Gardens. (p89)

Camera Obscura The outlook tower here provides an iconic view along the Royal Mile. (p52)

Castle Esplanade Commanding views north across the New Town, or south towards the Pentland Hills. (p37)

Best Restaurant Views

Tower Perched at the top of the National Museum of Scotland, with a superb view of the castle. (p59)

Maxie's Bistro Outdoor tables on Victoria Terrace look out over Victoria St to the Grassmarket. (p62)

Scottish Cafe & Restaurant The window tables here have a lovely outlook along Princes Street Gardens. (p103)

For Kids

Edinburgh has plenty of attractions for children, and most things to see and do are child friendly. During the Edinburgh and Fringe Festivals there's lots of street theatre for kids, especially on High St and at the foot of the Mound, and in December there's a Ferris wheel and fairground rides in Princes Street Gardens and an ice rink in St Andrew Sq.

LOU ARMOR/SHUTTERSTOCK ©

Best Sights for Kids

Edinburgh Castle Ask at the ticket office about the Children's Quiz, which lets kids track down various clues and treasures. (p36)

Edinburgh Zoo Giant pandas, interactive chimpanzee enclosure, penguins on parade... (p97; pictured)

Our Dynamic Earth Loads of great stuff, from earthquake simulators to real icebergs. (p80)

Camera Obscura Fascinating exhibits on illusions, magic tricks, electricity and holograms. (p52)

Real Mary King's Close Older children will enjoy the ghost stories and creepy atmosphere here. Children under five years not admitted. (p40)

Scott Monument Lots of narrow stairs to climb, grotesque carvings to spot and a view at the top. (p89)

Best Museums for Kids

National Museum of Scotland Lots of interactive exhibits, and trail leaflets for kids to follow and fill in. (p42)

Scottish National Gallery of Modern Art Great landscaped grounds for exploring – track down all the sculptures! (p112)

Top Tips

○ *Edinburgh for Under Fives* (www.efuf.co.uk) has a useful website and guidebook. *The List* (www.list.co.uk/kids) events guide has a kids section.

○ Up to two children under five may travel free on public transport when accompanied by a fare-paying adult. Children five to 15 pay half the adult fare.

Tours

/GETTY IMAGES ©

Best Walking Tours

City of the Dead Tours
(www.cityofthedeadtours.
com; adult/concession
£11/9; ⏰9pm Easter-Oct,
8.30pm Nov-Easter) This
tour of Greyfriars Kirkyard
is probably the scariest of
Edinburgh's 'ghost' tours.
Many people have reported
encounters with the McKenzie Poltergeist, the ghost of
a 17th-century judge who
persecuted the Covenanters,
and now haunts their former
prison in a corner of the
kirkyard (churchyard). Not
suitable for young children.

**Edinburgh Literary
Pub Tour** (www.edinburgh
literarypubtour.co.uk; adult/
student £14/10; ⏰7.30pm
daily May-Sep, limited days
Oct-Apr) An enlightening,
two-hour trawl through
Edinburgh's literary history
– and its associated howffs
(meeting places, often
pubs) – in the entertaining
company of Messrs Clart
and McBrain.

Mercat Tours (📞0131-
225 5445; www.mercat
tours.com; Mercat Cross;
adult/child £13/8; 🚌35)
Mercat offers a wide range
of fascinating history walks
and 'Ghosts & Ghouls' tours,
but its most famous is a
visit to the hidden, haunted,
underground vaults beneath
South Bridge.

**Cadies & Witchery
Tours** (📞0131-225 6745;
www.witcherytours.com;
84 West Bow; adult/child
£10/7.50; ⏰7pm year-
round, plus 9pm Apr-Sep;
🚌2) The becloaked and
pasty-faced Adam Lyal
(deceased) leads a Murder
& Mystery tour of the Old
Town's darker corners.

Rebus Tours (📞0131-
553 7473; www.rebustours.
com; per person £15;
⏰noon Sat) A two-hour
guided tour of the 'hidden
Edinburgh' frequented by
novelist Ian Rankin's fictional
detective, John Rebus. Not
recommended for children
under 10.

Invisible (Edinburgh)
(📞07500-773709; www.
invisible-cities.org; per
person £10) A new venture
that trains homeless people
as tour guides to explore
a different side of the city.
Tour themes include Crime
& Punishment (includes
Burke and Hare) and Powerful Women (from Maggie
Dickson to JK Rowling).
Must be booked in advance;
check website for times.

Best Bus Tour

Majestic Tour (www.
edinburghtour.com; adult/
child £15/7.50; ⏰daily
year-round except 25 Dec)
Hop-on/ hop-off tour
departing every 15 to 20
minutes from Waverley
Bridge to the Royal Yacht
Britannia at Ocean Ter-
minal via the New Town,
Royal Botanic Garden and
Newhaven, returning via
Leith Walk, Holyrood and the
Royal Mile.

Activities

Edinburgh has plenty of places to perk up your sagging muscles with a spot of healthy exercise. Hikers can head for the Holyrood Park or Hermitage of Braid, cyclists can take advantage of the city's network of cycle paths, and golfers can take their pick from around 90 courses within easy reach of the city.

JAROSLAV MORAVCIK/SHUTTERSTOCK ©

Best for Walking

Arthur's Seat Hike to the summit for outstanding views. (p79; pictured)

Holyrood Park Jog around Arthur's Seat through this little bit of wilderness in the heart of the city. (p80)

Hermitage of Braid Enjoy a rural walk along this lovely wooded glen. (p151)

Best for Cycling

Water of Leith Walkway (www.waterofleith.org. uk) Runs from the sea at Leith to the Pentland Hills southwest of the city.

Innocent Railway A dedicated cycle path running from the southern side of Arthur's Seat eastwards to Musselburgh (5 miles) and on to Ormiston and Pencaitland.

Best for Golfing

Braid Hills Public Golf Course (www.edinburgh leisure.co.uk/venues/braid-hills-golf-course) Take in a round of golf on this scenic, but challenging, course.

Duddingston Golf Course (www.duddingstongolfclub. co.uk) Enjoy playing in a picturesque setting beneath Arthur's Seat.

Leith Links Visit the place where the rules of golf were formalised in 1744. (p139)

Top Tips

o The **Scottish Rights of Way & Access Society** (☎ 0131-558 1222; www.scotways.com) provides information and advice on walking trails and rights of way in Scotland.

o For details of golf courses in and around Edinburgh, check out www.scottish golfcourses.com.

o Hybrid bikes, road bikes and Brompton folding bikes can be rented from Biketrax (p165).

Four Perfect Days

Day 1

Spend the first two hours of the morning at **Edinburgh Castle** (p36), then stroll down the Royal Mile, stopping off for a pre-booked tour of the historic **Real Mary King's Close** (p40).

At the bottom of the Mile, take a one-hour guided tour of the **Scottish Parliament Building** (p74), before crossing the street to the **Palace of Holyroodhouse** (p72). Then, if the weather's fine, head up the stairs from nearby Calton Rd to the summit of **Calton Hill** (p97; pictured) for superb views across the city.

Before or after dinner, scare yourself silly on a ghost tour of **Greyfriars Kirkyard** (p55), then head to the **Bongo Club** (p62) or **Cabaret Voltaire** (p62) for some alternative-style entertainment.

Day 2

Make morning number two a feast of culture, with a tour of the **National Museum of Scotland** (p42), followed by a stroll down the Mound to the **Scottish National Gallery** (p96).

Climb to the top of the **Scott Monument** (p89; pictured) for panoramic views, then catch a bus from Princes St to Ocean Terminal for a visit to the **Royal Yacht Britannia** (p136). Time your trip to get the last two hours of opening here.

Stay in Leith for a pint at **Teuchters Landing** (p144) or a cocktail in a teapot at the **Roseleaf** (p142), or head back to the city centre to sample some Edinburgh-brewed beer in the magnificent surroundings of the **Café Royal Circle Bar** (p103).

Day 3

Begin with a visit to the **Scottish National Gallery of Modern Art** (p112), then enjoy a walk along the Water of Leith Walkway to Stockbridge, where you can explore the boutiques on St Stephen St before pausing for lunch.

If it's Sunday, browse the stalls at **Stockbridge Market** (p132), then make the short stroll to the **Royal Botanic Garden** (p124; pictured). This is one of the UK's leading gardens, so devote the rest of the afternoon to exploring the palm houses, rock gardens, woodland gardens and outdoor sculptures.

Have tickets booked for a show at the **Royal Lyceum** (p120) or the **Traverse** (p120), or else head for late-night traditional Scottish music and dancing at **Ghillie Dhu** (p118).

Day 4

Head to the southern fringes of the city and devote the morning to the *Da Vinci Code* delights of **Rosslyn Chapel** (p158). This 15th-century church is a monument to the stonemason's art.

Return to the city centre to spend the afternoon browsing the New Town shops and visiting the **Scottish National Portrait Gallery** (p86; pictured), which leads you through Scottish history via portraits of famous personalities. Take an early-evening stroll through **Princes Street Gardens** (p88), then wander down Leith Walk to **Joseph Pearce's** (p104) for a gin and tonic before dinner.

Round off the evening with some live jazz at the **Jam House** (p107), or a comedy act at **The Stand** (p108).

Need to Know

For detailed information, see Survival Guide p161

Currency
Pound sterling (£); 100 pence = £1

Language
English

Visas
Generally not needed for stays of up to six months. Not a member of the Schengen Zone. (Note: this may change following the UK's departure from the EU in 2019.)

Money
ATMs widespread. Major credit cards accepted everywhere.

Mobile Phones
Uses the GSM 900/1800 network. Local SIM cards can be used in European and Australian phones.

Time
Edinburgh is on GMT; during British Summer Time (BST; last Sunday in March to last Saturday in October) clocks are one hour ahead of GMT.

Daily Budget

Budget: Less than £50

Dorm bed: £15–30

Lunch special or food shopping at market: £5–10

Many museums and galleries: free

Midrange: £50–150

Double room: £80–100

Two-course dinner with glass of wine: £30

Live music in pub: free–£10

Top End: More than £150

Double room in boutique/four-star hotel: £175–225

Three-course dinner (including wine) in top restaurant: £70–100

Taxi across town: £15

Advance Planning

Six months before Book accommodation for the August festival period. Book a table at the Witchery by the Castle restaurant (p59).

Two months before Book hotel or B&B accommodation; reserve tables in top restaurants; book car hire.

One month before Buy tickets online for Edinburgh Castle (p36); check listings for theatre, live music etc and book tickets.

Arriving in Edinburgh

Most visitors arrive at Edinburgh Airport (www.edinburghairport.com), 8 miles west of the city centre, or at Edinburgh Waverley train station, right in the heart of the city between the Old Town and New Town.

✈ Edinburgh Airport

Bus 100 runs from the airport to Waverley Bridge (30 minutes) every 10 minutes from 4am to midnight and every 30 minutes through the night. Trams run from the airport to the city centre (33 minutes, every six to eight minutes from 6am to midnight). An airport taxi to the city centre takes about 30 minutes.

🚆 Waverley Train Station

Taxi rank in station. Short walk to Princes St, where trams and buses depart to all areas of the city.

Getting Around

🚌 Bus

Best way of getting from the suburbs to the centre, and for north–south trips. Despite dedicated bus lanes, buses can get held up during rush hours.

🚋 Tram

Fast and frequent service from the airport to York Place in the east of the city centre, via Murrayfield Stadium, Haymarket, the West End and Princes St.

🚗 Taxi

Great for late-night journeys, but fares can be expensive unless there are four people sharing.

🚲 Bike

Hire a bike and escape to the countryside via the Water of Leith Walkway, or the Union Canal towpath.

Edinburgh Neighbourhoods

Stockbridge (p123)
A former village with its own distinct identity, stylish and quirky shops and a good choice of pubs and restaurants.

New Town (p85)
Georgian terraces lined with designer boutiques, wine bars and cocktail lounges, plus Princes Street Gardens and the perfect viewpoint of Calton Hill.

West End & Dean Village (p111)
More Georgian elegance and upmarket shops, leading down to the picturesque Dean Village in the wooded valley of the Water of Leith.

South Edinburgh (p147)
A peaceful residential area of Victorian tenement flats and spacious garden villa; not much in the way of tourist attractions, but good walking territory and many good restaurants and pubs.

Royal Botanic Garden

Scottish National Portrait Gallery

Scottish National Gallery of Modern Art

Princes Street Gardens

Real Mary King's Close

Edinburgh Castle

Leith (p135)
Redeveloped industrial docklands now occupied by restaurants, bars and Ocean Terminal, the city's biggest shopping centre.

Royal Yacht Britannia

Holyrood & Arthur's Seat (p71)
At the foot of the Royal Mile, contains the Scottish Parliament and the Palace of Holyroodhuose, and is the gateway to the craggy parkland of Arthur's Seat.

Scottish Parliament Building **Palace of Holyroodhouse**

National Museum of Scotland

Old Town (p35)
A maze of narrow wynds (alleys) and cobbled streets, strung out along the Royal Mile, home to the city's main historical sights.

Explore
Edinburgh

Colourful Victoria Street, Old Town (p35) JAMES HEATLIE/SHUTTERSTOCK ©

Explore
Old Town

Edinburgh's Old Town is a jagged, jumbled maze of historic masonry riddled with closes, stairs, vaults and wynds (narrow alleys) leading off the cobbled ravine of the Royal Mile, which links Edinburgh Castle to the Palace of Holyroodhouse. The restored 16th- and 17th-century Old Town tenements support a thriving city-centre community, crammed at street level with museums, restaurants, bars and shops.

Be at Edinburgh Castle (p36) for opening time, and plan on spending two hours exploring its many attractions before heading downhill along the Royal Mile, stopping off as the fancy takes you at the Scotch Whisky Experience (p52) and the Camera Obscura (p52) before enjoying a seafood lunch at Ondine (p56). Join a tour of the Real Mary King's Close (p40) then spend the rest of the afternoon at the National Museum of Scotland (p42). Get your photo taken beside the statue of Greyfriars Bobby (p55) before heading down to the Grassmarket (p47) for a drink, then dinner with a view at the Tower (p59).

Getting There & Around

🚍 Service 300 runs along the lower part of the Royal Mile from South Bridge to the Palace of Holyroodhouse; bus 6 links Hanover St in the New Town to the Scottish Parliament Building via Market St, St Mary's St and Holyrood Rd. Buses 23, 27, 41, 42 and 67 run along the Mound and George IV Bridge.

Neighbourhood Map on p50

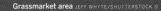

Grassmarket area JEFF WHYTE/SHUTTERSTOCK ©

Top Sight 📷
Edinburgh Castle

The brooding black crags of Castle Rock, rising above the western end of Princes St, are the very reason for Edinburgh's existence. This rocky hill was the most easily defended hilltop on the invasion route between England and central Scotland. Today it is one of Scotland's most atmospheric and popular tourist attractions.

⊙ MAP P50, A4

www.edinburghcastle.
gov.uk

Castle Esplanade

adult/child £18.50/11.50,
audioguide £3.50/£1.50

🕘9.30am-6pm Apr-Sep,
to 5pm Oct-Mar, last entry
1hr before closing

🚌23, 27, 41, 42, 67

The Esplanade

The castle's Esplanade is a parade ground dating from 1820, with superb views south over the city towards the Pentland Hills. At its western end is the **Entrance Gateway**, dating from 1888 and flanked by statues of Robert the Bruce and William Wallace. Above the gate is the Royal Standard of Scotland – a red lion rampant on a gold field – and the Scottish royal motto in Latin, 'Nemo me impune lacessit'. This translates into Scots as 'wha daur meddle wi' me', and into English as 'watch it, pal' (OK, it literally means 'no one provokes me with impunity').

One O'Clock Gun

Inside the entrance a cobbled lane leads up beneath the 16th-century **Portcullis Gate**, topped by the 19th-century **Argyle Tower**, and past the cannon of the Argyle and Mills Mount Batteries. The battlements here have great views over the New Town to the Firth of Forth. At the far end of Mills Mount Battery is the One O'Clock Gun, a gleaming WWII 25-pounder that fires an ear-splitting time signal at 1pm every day (except Sunday, Christmas Day and Good Friday).

St Margaret's Chapel

South of Mills Mount the road curls up leftward through **Foog's Gate** to the highest part of Castle Rock, crowned by the tiny St Margaret's Chapel, the oldest surviving building in Edinburgh. It's a simple Romanesque structure that was probably built by David I or Alexander I in memory of their mother, Queen Margaret, sometime around 1130 (she was canonised in 1250). Following Cromwell's capture of the castle in 1650 it was used to store ammunition until it was restored at the order of Queen Victoria; it was rededicated in 1934. The tiny stained-glass windows – depicting Margaret, St Andrew, St Columba, St Ninian and William Wallace – date from the 1920s.

★ Top Tips

o Avoid ticket-office queues by purchasing your tickets online via the Edinburgh Castle website.

o It's worth hiring an audioguide (£3.50) to provide extra context for the various historical attractions you will see.

o Time your visit to coincide with the firing of the One O'Clock Gun.

✕ Take a Break

The **Tea Rooms at Edinburgh Castle** (www.edinburghcastle. scot/shop-eat/cafes; Crown Sq; mains £9-15; ⏰ 9.30am-5pm Apr-Oct, 10.30am-4pm Nov-Mar; ♿ ; 🚍 23, 27, 41, 42) serves good lunches.

Just a few yards downhill from the castle on the Royal Mile, there's Cannonball Restaurant (p57) for top-quality Scottish cuisine.

Mons Meg

Immediately north of St Margaret's Chapel is Mons Meg, a giant 15th-century siege gun built at Mons in Belgium in 1449. The gun was last fired in 1681, as a birthday salute for the future James VII/II, when its barrel burst. Take a peek over the wall to the north of the chapel and you'll see a charming little garden that was used as a **pet cemetery** for officers' dogs.

Great Hall

The main group of buildings on the summit of Castle Rock are ranged around Crown Sq, dominated by the shrine of the **Scottish National War Memorial**. Opposite is the Great Hall, built for James IV (r 1488–1513) as a ceremonial hall

and used as a meeting place for the Scottish Parliament until 1639. Its most remarkable feature is the original 16th-century hammer-beam roof.

Prisons of War Exhibition

The **Castle Vaults** beneath the Great Hall (entered on the west side of Crown Sq) were used variously as storerooms, bakeries and prisons. The vaults have been restored to how they were in the 18th and early 19th centuries, when they were used as a prison for soldiers captured during the American War of Independence and the Napoleonic Wars. Original graffiti carved by French and American prisoners can be seen on the ancient wooden doors.

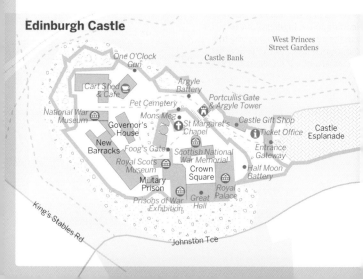

Edinburgh Castle

The Stone of Destiny

On St Andrew's Day 1996, with much pomp and circumstance, a block of sandstone 26.5 inches by 16.5 inches by 11 inches in size (67cm by 42cm by 28cm), with rusted iron hoops at either end, was installed in Edinburgh Castle. For the previous 700 years it had lain beneath the Coronation Chair in London's Westminster Abbey, where almost every English – and later British – monarch from Edward II in 1308 to Elizabeth II in 1953 had sat during their coronation ceremonies.

This is the legendary Stone of Destiny, on which Scottish kings placed their feet (not their bums; the English got that bit wrong) during their coronation. It was stolen from Scone Abbey near Perth by Edward I of England in 1296 and taken to London, where it remained for seven centuries, an enduring symbol of Scotland's subjugation by England.

It returned to the political limelight in 1996, when the Westminster government arranged for its return in an attempt to boost the flagging popularity of the Conservative Party in Scotland prior to a general election. (The stunt failed: Scotland returned no Conservative MPs at the ensuing election.)

Honours of Scotland

The **Royal Palace**, built during the 15th and 16th centuries, houses a series of historical tableaux leading to the highlight of the castle: a strongroom housing the Honours of Scotland (the Scottish crown jewels), the oldest surviving crown jewels in Europe. Locked away in a chest following the *Act of Union* in 1707, the crown (made in 1540 from the gold of Robert the Bruce's 14th-century coronet), sword and sceptre lay forgotten until they were unearthed at the instigation of novelist Sir Walter Scott in 1818. Also on display here is the **Stone of Destiny**.

Among the neighbouring **Royal Apartments** is the bedchamber where Mary, Queen of Scots, gave birth to her son James VI, who was to unite the crowns of Scotland and England in 1603.

Top Sight 📷
Real Mary King's Close

Edinburgh's 18th-century city chambers were
built over the sealed-off remains of Mary King's
Close, and the lower levels of this medieval Old
Town alley have survived almost unchanged amid
the foundations for 250 years. Now open to the
public, this spooky, subterranean labyrinth gives
a fascinating insight into the everyday life of 17th-
century Edinburgh.

◉ MAP P50, D3

📞 0131-225 0672

www.realmarykingsclose.com

2 Warriston's Close

adult/child £15.50/9.50

🕒 hours vary

🚌 23, 27, 41, 42

The Tenement Room

A drama student in period costume will take you on a guided tour through the vaults while practising his or her dramatic enunciation and corny jokes. The scripted tour, complete with ghostly tales and gruesome tableaux, can seem a little naff, milking the scary and scatological aspects of the close's history for all they're worth. But there are things of genuine interest to see: there's something about the crumbling 17th-century tenement room that makes the hair rise on the back of your neck, with tufts of horsehair poking from collapsing lath-and-plaster walls that bear the ghost of a pattern, and the ancient smell of stone and dust thick in your nostrils.

Wee Annie's Room

In one of the former bedrooms off the close, a psychic once claimed to have been approached by the ghost of a little girl called Annie. It's hard to tell what's more frightening – the story of the ghostly child, or the bizarre heap of tiny dolls and teddies left in a corner by sympathetic visitors.

The Foot of the Close

Perhaps the most atmospheric part of the tour is at the end, when you stand at the foot of Mary King's Close itself. You are effectively standing in a buried street, with the old tenement walls rising on either side, and the weight of the 11 storeys of the city chambers above – and some 250 years of history – pressing down all around you.

★ Top Tips

o Tours are limited to 20 people at a time, so book online at least 24 hours in advance to secure a place.

o The tour includes a lot of stairs and uneven stone surfaces – wear suitable shoes.

o There are lots of enclosed spaces – not recommended if you suffer from claustrophobia!

o Children under the age of five are not admitted.

✗ Take a Break

Enjoy pizza at a pavement table at **Gordon's Trattoria** (☎ 0131-225 7992; www.gordons trattoria.com; 231 High St; mains £12-23; ☉ noon-11pm Sun-Thu, to midnight Fri & Sat; ⛹; ☒ all South Bridge buses), a short distance downhill.

For a more sophisticated seafood lunch, head to Ondine (p56), uphill and round the corner.

Top Sight

National Museum of Scotland

*The golden stone and striking modern archi-
tecture of the National Museum's new building
(1998) make it one of the city's most distinctive
landmarks. The building's five floors trace the
history of Scotland from geological beginnings to
the 1990s, and connect with the original Victorian
museum, which covers natural history, world
cultures, archaeology, design and fashion, and
science and technology.*

◎ MAP P50, E5

www.nms.ac.uk/national-
museum-of-scotland

Chambers St

admission free

🕙 10am-5pm

🚻

🚌 45, 300

Grand Gallery

The museum's main entrance, in the middle of Chambers St, leads into an atmospheric entrance hall occupying what used to be the museum cellars. Stairs lead up into the light of the Victorian Grand Gallery (pictured left), a spectacular glass-roofed atrium lined with cast-iron pillars and balconies; this was the centrepiece of the original Victorian museum. It was designed in the 1860s by Captain Francis Fowke of the Royal Engineers, who also created the Royal Albert Hall in London, and parts of London's Victoria and Albert Museum.

Crowds gather on the hour to watch the chiming of the **Millennium Clock Tower**. Built in 1999 to commemorate the best and worst of human history, and inspired by mechanical marvels such as Prague's Astronomical Clock, it is more a kinetic sculpture than a clock, crammed with amusing and thought-provoking symbols and animated figures.

Animal World

A door at the eastern end of the Grand Gallery leads into Animal World, one of the most impressive of the old building's exhibits. No dusty, static regiments of stuffed creatures here, but a beautiful and dynamic display of animals apparently caught in the act of leaping, flying or swimming, arranged in groups that illustrate different means of locomotion, methods of feeding and modes of reproduction. Extinct creatures, including a full-size skeleton of a Tyrannosaurus rex, mingle with the extant.

Window on the World

The exhibits ranged around the balconies of the Grand Gallery are billed as a 'Window on the World', showcasing more than 800 items from the museum's collections, ranging from the **world's largest scrimshaw carving**, occupying

★ Top Tips

o Begin at the main entrance in the middle of Chambers St, rather than the modern tower at the western end of the street. You'll find an info desk with museum maps and leaflets, a cloakroom, toilets and a cafe-restaurant.

o Free, one-hour guided tours of the museum depart at 11am, 1pm and 3pm, each covering a different theme; ask for details at the info desk.

o You can download PDFs of museum trails for children to follow and a National Museum of Scotland Highlights app for iOS and Android.

✗ Take a Break

The **Museum Brasserie** (📞 0131-225 4040; www.benugo. com/restaurants/ museum-brasserie; Chambers St; mains £9-14; ⏱10am-5pm; 👶; 🚌 45, 300) in the basement of the Victorian part of the museum serves light lunches.

two full-size sperm-whale jawbones, to a four-seat racing bicycle dating from 1898.

Hawthornden Court

A suite of science and technology galleries link the Grand Gallery of the old museum to Hawthornden Court in the new building, with exhibits that include Dolly the sheep, the first mammal ever to be cloned, historic aircraft, and a section of a particle accelerator from CERN (European Organization for Nuclear Research).

Early People Gallery

Stairs at the far end of Hawthornden Court lead down to the Early People Gallery on Level 0, decorated with intriguing humanoid sculptures by Sir Eduardo Paolozzi and beautiful installations by sculptor Andy Goldsworthy, including huge stacks of old roofing slates, cleverly arranged scrap timber and a sphere made entirely of whale bones. Look out for the **Cramond Lioness**, a Roman funerary sculpture of a lion gripping a human head in her jaws (it was discovered in the River Almond, on the western edge of Edinburgh, in 1997), and the 22kg of Roman silver that makes up the **Traprain Treasure**. It was buried in the 5th century AD and discovered in 1919, and is the biggest known hoard of Roman silver ever to be found.

Kingdom of the Scots

From the Early People Gallery you work your way upwards through the history of Scotland. Highlights of the medieval Kingdom of the Scots

Tyrannosaurus rex life-sized skeleton cast

galleries, on Levels 1 and 2, include the **Monymusk Reliquary**, a tiny silver casket dating from AD 750, which is said to have been carried into battle with Robert the Bruce at Bannockburn in 1314; and the famous **Lewis chessmen**, charming 12th-century chess pieces carved from walrus ivory, that were discovered on Uig beach on the Isle of Lewis.

Death Comes In...

The Daith Comes In (Death Comes In) exhibit on Level 4 is a goth's paradise of wooden hearses, jet jewellery, and mourning bracelets made from human hair, as well as the 'mortsafes' that once protected newly buried corpses from the ravages of the body snatchers (p55). But the most fascinating objects on display here are the mysterious **Arthur's Seat coffins**. Discovered in a cave in 1836 by some boys hunting rabbits, these miniature coffins (only eight of the original 17 survive) are less than 10cm long and have tiny wooden figures inside. They may have been part of a mock burial for the victims of Edinburgh's most famous body snatchers, Burke and Hare, who sold their murdered victims to the city's anatomy professor.

Leaving Scotland

Level 6 of the museum is given over to the 20th century, with galleries devoted to war, industry and daily life illustrated by personal stories, film clips and iconic objects such as a **set of bagpipes** that was played at the Battle of the Somme in 1916. There is also an exhibition called Leaving Scotland, containing stories of the Scottish diaspora that emigrated to begin new lives in Canada, Australia, the USA and other places, from the 18th century right up until the 1960s.

Roof Terrace

Before you leave, find the elevator in the corner of Level 6, near the war gallery, and go up to the roof terrace to enjoy a fantastic view across the city to the castle ramparts.

Walking Tour 🥾

Explore the Old Town's Hidden History

Edinburgh's Old Town extends to the south of the Royal Mile, descending into the valley of the Grassmarket and Cowgate, which is crossed by the arches of George IV Bridge and South Bridge. This difference in levels has created a maze of narrow closes, wynds and staircases, which lend an adventurous air to exploring its many hidden corners.

Walk Facts

Start Victoria Terrace
End South Bridge Vaults
Length 1.5 miles; one hour

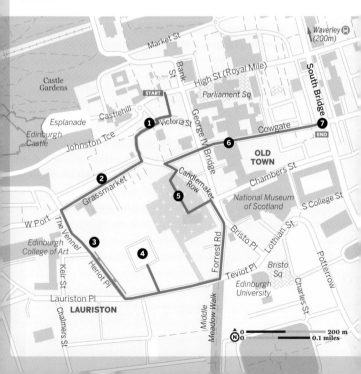

❶ Victoria Terrace

From the Lawnmarket at the top of the Royal Mile, dive down Fisher's Close, which leads you onto the delightful Victoria Terrace, strung above the cobbled curve of shop-lined Victoria St. Wander along to the right, enjoying the view – **Maxie's Bistro** (p62), at the far end of the terrace, is a great place to stop for lunch or a drink.

❷ Grassmarket

Descend the stairs in the middle of the terrace and continue downhill to the Grassmarket. The site of a cattle market from the 15th century until the start of the 20th, the Grassmarket was also the city's place of execution, and martyred Covenanters are commemorated by a monument at the eastern end, where the gallows once stood. The notorious murderers Burke and Hare operated from a now-vanished close off the west end.

❸ Flodden Wall

Turn left up the flight of stairs known as the Vennel. At the top of the steps on the left you'll find the Flodden Wall, one of the few surviving fragments of the city wall that was built in the early 16th century as protection against a feared English invasion. Beyond it stretches the Telfer Wall, a later extension.

❹ George Heriot's School

Turn left along Lauriston Pl to find George Heriot's School, one of the most impressive buildings in the Old Town. Built in the 17th century with funds bequeathed by George Heriot (goldsmith and banker to King James VI, and popularly known as Jinglin' Geordie), it was originally a school for orphaned children, but became a fee-paying school in 1886.

❺ Greyfriar's Kirkyard

Hemmed in by high walls and overlooked by the castle, Greyfriars Kirkyard is one of Edinburgh's most evocative spots, a peaceful green oasis dotted with elaborate monuments. Many famous Edinburgh names are buried here, including poet Allan Ramsay (1686–1758) and William Smellie (1740–95), editor of the first edition of *Encyclopaedia Britannica*.

❻ Cowgate

The Cowgate – the long, dark ravine leading eastward from the Grassmarket – was once the road along which cattle were driven from the pastures around Arthur's Seat to the safety of the city walls, or to be sold at market. To the right are the new law courts, followed by Tailors Hall (built 1621, extended 1757), now a hotel and bar but formerly the meeting place of the 'Companie of Tailzeours' (Tailors' Guild).

❼ South Bridge Vaults

South Bridge passes over the Cowgate in a single arch, but there are another nine arches hidden on either side, surrounded by later buildings. The ones to the north can be visited on a guided tour with **Mercat Tours** (p24); those to the south are occupied by a nightclub, **Caves** (p65).

Walking Tour 🥾

From Castle to Palace

Edinburgh Castle, the Palace of Holyroodhouse and the Scottish Parliament are what make Edinburgh Scotland's capital. This walk links the city's most iconic sights by following (mostly) the Royal Mile, the ancient processional route followed by kings and queens travelling between castle and palace.

Walk Facts

Start Edinburgh Castle

End Palace of Holyroodhouse

Length 1.5 miles; one hour

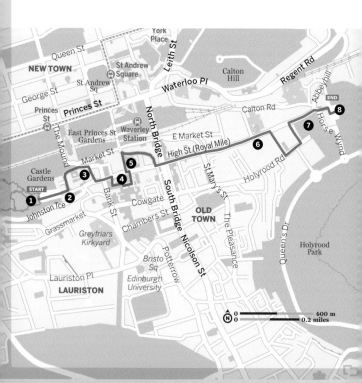

❶ Edinburgh Castle

Dominating the city from its superb defensive position, **Edinburgh Castle** (p36) is one of Britain's most impressive fortresses. Check out the Scottish Crown Jewels, wander through the former prisons in the Castle Vaults, and try not to jump when the One O'Clock Gun is fired.

❷ Scotch Whisky Experience

After enjoying the views from the **Castle Esplanade**, head down the Royal Mile. On the left you'll pass the **Witches Well** (a fountain commemorating those executed on suspicion of witchcraft) before reaching the **Scotch Whisky Experience** (p52).

❸ Writers' Museum

Descend Ramsay Lane to the twin towers of Edinburgh's **New College**, and see the **statue of John Knox** in the courtyard. Return to the Royal Mile via **Lady Stair's Close**, a picturesque Old Town alley, and the **Writers' Museum** (p53).

❹ St Giles Cathedral

Continue down the High St to **St Giles Cathedral** (p52), Edinburgh's most important church. Follow Parliament Sq around the south side of the church, and take a look at **Parliament Hall** and the **Mercat Cross**.

❺ Real Mary King's Close

Back on the High St is the Georgian facade of the **city chambers** (seat of Edinburgh city council), which was built over a medieval Old Town alley with eerie remains you can explore on a tour of the **Real Mary King's Close** (p40).

❻ Museum of Edinburgh

Descend **Advocate's Close**, one of the most atmospheric of the Old Town's wynds, then climb back to the Royal Mile along **Cockburn St**, lined with trendy boutiques. Continue down the High St, past **John Knox House** (p54), to the **Museum of Edinburgh** (p52).

❼ Scottish Parliament Building

Opposite **Canongate Kirk**, go down Crighton's Close past the **Scottish Poetry Library**, then left and left again up Reid's Close, to see the **Scottish Parliament Building** (p74).

❽ Palace of Holyroodhouse

The Royal Mile ends at the ornate gates of the **Palace of Holyroodhouse** (p72), the official residence of the royal family when they're in town.

For reviews see
- ◉ Top Sights p36
- ◉ Sights p52
- ✕ Eating p56
- 🍷 Drinking p62
- ★ Entertainment p65
- 🔒 Shopping p67

A
B
C
D

1

St Andrew Square

George St

St Andrew Sq

NEW TOWN

S St Andrew St

Rose St

Hanover St

S St David St

Princes St

2

Frederick St

Princes St

Scott Monument

Edinburgh Tour Offi

Princes St

Royal Scottish Academy

East Princes St Gardens

Waverley Bridge

Princes St

Scottish National Gallery

The Mound

Underground Solush'n

3

Market St

Real Ma King's Clos

Writers' Museum

N Bank St

Bank St

S St Giles St

44 🔒 Merca Tour

Mound Pl

James Ct

◉ 6

St Giles Cathedral ◉ 1

West Princes St Gardens

Ramsay La

Gladstone's Land

35 ✕ ◉ 5

Lawnmarket

George IV Bridge

Parliament Ha

Camera Obscura & World of Illusions

4 ◉

Castlehill

22 ✕

15 ✕

National Library of Scotland

4

Edinburgh Castle ◉

16 ✕ ◉ 3 ✕ 21

Esplanade

Scotch Whisky Experience

25 ✕

✕ 26

Victoria St

34

Central Library

28 ◉

Johnston Tce

45 🔒

52 🔒

Candlemaker Row

46 🔒

Merchant St

Sher Cou

43 🔒

Grassmarket

Heriot Bridge

Greyfriars Kirkyard ◉ 10

51 🔒

Greyfriars Bobby Statue ◉ 11 ◉ 20

5

King's Stables Rd

King's Stables La

48 🔒

W Port

Greyfriars Kirk ◉ 9

Forrest Rd

Bris

◉ 4 ◉ 17

Edinburgh College of Art

George Heriot's School

Telfer Wall

Heriot Pl

Teviot

6

Lady Lawson St

Keir St

Lauriston Pl

Lauriston Pl

LAURISTON

Lauriston Pl

Lauriston St

A
B
C
D

E
F
G
H

Leith St

Waterloo Pl

St Andrew's House

Calton Hill

Royal High School

1

Regent Rd

North Bridge

Calton Rd

Calton Rd

Old Tolbooth Wynd

Canongate Kirkyard

2

Waverley Station

P

E Market St

New St

●12

People's **8**
Story

●2
Museum of
Edinburgh

ty Art
entre Market St

Jeffrey St

Cranston St

John Knox
House

Canongate (Royal Mile)

okie Pie in
● the Sky

Cockburn
St

49 🔒●7

19

🔒✕18
47

St John St

3

Museum
Context

High St (Royal Mile)

🔒
53

St Mary's St

Holyrood Rd

41
●

Niddry St

Blackfriars St

S Gray's Cl

23
✕
●33

Old Fishmarket Cl

✕24
Tron Sq

27

40

●30

St John's
Hill

4

Pleasance
Sports Centre

Viewcraig Gdns

Cowgate

37

●29

Guthrie
St

39

South Bridge

Blair St

38
Infirmary St

●13
Edinburgh
University
Campus

Drummond St

Viewcraig St

OLD TOWN

Chambers St

Dovecot
Studios

50

Edinburgh
University

Roxburgh Pl

E Adam St

5

W College St

S College St

Surgeons'
Hall
Museums

The Pleasance

National
Museum of
Scotland

Edinburgh
Festival
Theatre

Hill Pl

31 32
● ●

Potterrow

W Richmond St

Brown St

risto Pl Lothian St

Holyrood
Park

Bristo Sq

Marshall
St

Nicolson Sq

Nicolson St

Davie St

6

Edinburgh
University

N
0   200 m
0   0.1 miles

E
F
G
H

Sights

St Giles Cathedral CHURCH

1 ⊙ MAP P50, D3

The great grey bulk of St Giles Cathedral dates largely from the 15th century, but much of it was restored in the 19th century. One of the most interesting corners of the kirk is the **Thistle Chapel**, built in 1911 for the Knights of the Most Ancient & Most Noble Order of the Thistle. The elaborately carved Gothic-style stalls have canopies topped with the helms and arms of the 16 knights – look out for the bagpipe-playing angel amid the vaulting. (www.stgilescathedral.org.uk; High St; admission free; ⏰9am-7pm Mon-Fri, to 5pm Sat, 1-5pm Sun Apr-Oct, 9am-5pm Mon-Sat, 1-5pm Sun Nov-Mar; 🚌23, 27, 41, 42)

Museum of Edinburgh MUSEUM

2 ⊙ MAP P50, H2

You can't miss the colourful facade of Huntly House, brightly painted in red and yellow ochre, opposite the Tollbooth clock on the Royal Mile. Built in 1570, it houses a museum covering Edinburgh from prehistory to the present. Exhibits of national importance include an original copy of the National Covenant of 1638, but the big crowd-pleaser is the dog collar and feeding bowl that once belonged to Greyfriars Bobby (p55), the city's most famous canine citizen. (☎0131-529 4143; www.edinburgh

museums.org.uk; 142 Canongate; admission free; ⏰10am-5pm Mon & Thu-Sat, noon-5pm Sun; 🚌300)

Scotch Whisky Experience MUSEUM

3 ⊙ MAP P50, B4

A former school houses this multimedia centre that takes you through the making of whisky, from barley to bottle, in a series of exhibits, demonstrations and talks that combine sight, sound and smell, including the world's largest collection of malt whiskies (3384 bottles!). The pricier tours include extensive whisky tastings and samples of Scottish cuisine. There's also a restaurant (p61) that serves traditional Scottish dishes with, where possible, a dash of whisky thrown in. (www.scotch whiskyexperience.co.uk; 354 Castlehill; adult/child from £15.50/7.50; ⏰10am-6pm Apr-Jul, to 5pm Aug-Mar; 🚌23, 27, 41, 42)

Camera Obscura & World of Illusions MUSEUM

4 ⊙ MAP P50, C4

Edinburgh's camera obscura is a curious 19th-century device – in constant use since 1853 – that uses lenses and mirrors to throw a live image of the city onto a large horizontal screen. The accompanying commentary is entertaining and the whole experience has a quirky charm, complemented by an intriguing exhibition dedicated to illusions of all kinds. Stairs lead up through various displays to the

Outlook Tower, which offers great views over the city. (www.camera-obscura.co.uk; Castlehill; adult/child £15.50/11.50; ⏱9am-10pm Jul & Aug, 9.30am-8pm Apr-Jun, Sep & Oct, 10am-7pm Nov-Mar; 🚍23, 27, 41, 42, 67)

Gladstone's Land
HISTORIC BUILDING

5 ◎ MAP P50, C3

One of Edinburgh's most prominent 17th-century merchants was Thomas Gledstanes, who in 1617 purchased the tenement later known as Gladstone's Land. It contains fine painted ceilings, walls and beams, and some splendid furniture from the 17th and 18th centuries. The guided tours (phone to book) provide a wealth of anecdotes and a detailed history. (NTS; 📞0131-226 5856; www.nts.org.uk/visit/places/gladstones-land; 477 Lawnmarket; adult/child £10/5; ⏱by prebooked guided tour; 🚍23, 27, 41, 42, 67)

Writers' Museum
MUSEUM

6 ◎ MAP P50, C3

Tucked down a close between the Royal Mile and the Mound you'll find Lady Stair's House (1622), home to this museum that contains manuscripts and memorabilia belonging to three of Scotland's most famous writers: Robert Burns, Sir Walter Scott and Robert Louis Stevenson. (📞0131-529 4901; www.edinburghmuseums.org.uk; Lady Stair's Close; admission free; ⏱10am-5pm Wed-Sat, noon-5pm Sun Aug; 🚍23, 27, 41, 42)

St Giles Cathedral

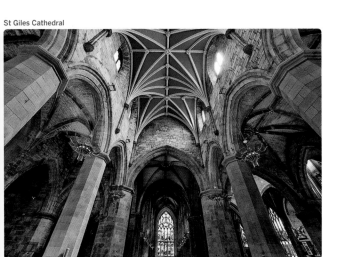

Ghost Tours

The **City of the Dead** (www.cityofthedeadtours.com; adult/concession £11/9; 9pm Easter-Oct, 8.30pm Nov-Easter) tour of Greyfriars Kirkyard is probably the scariest of Edinburgh's ghost tours. Many people have reported encounters with the McKenzie Poltergeist, the ghost of a 17th-century judge who persecuted the Covenanters (supporters of the Scottish Presbyterian church, in defiance of King Charles I's attempts to impose Roman Catholicism) and now haunts their former prison in a corner of the kirkyard. Not suitable for young children!

John Knox House   HISTORIC BUILDING

7 ⊙ MAP P50, F3

The Royal Mile narrows at the foot of High St beside the jutting facade of John Knox House. This is the oldest surviving tenement in Edinburgh, dating from around 1490. John Knox, an influential church reformer and leader of the Protestant Reformation in Scotland, is thought to have lived here from 1561 to 1572. The labyrinthine interior has some beautiful painted-timber ceilings and an interesting display on Knox's life and work. (www.tracscotland.org/scottish-storytelling-centre/john-knox-house-step-inside-history; 43-45 High St; adult/child £5/1; 10am-6pm Mon-Sat year-round, plus 10am-6pm Sun Jul & Aug; 35)

People's Story   MUSEUM

8 ⊙ MAP P50, H2

One of the surviving symbols of the Canongate district's former independence is the **Canongate Tollbooth**. Built in 1591, it served successively as a collection point for tolls (taxes), a council house, a courtroom and a jail. With picturesque turrets and a projecting clock, it's an interesting example of 16th-century architecture. It now houses a fascinating museum called the People's Story, which covers the life, work and pastimes of ordinary Edinburgh folk from the 18th century to today. (www.edinburghmuseums.org.uk; 163 Canongate; admission free; 10am-5pm Wed-Sat, noon-5pm Sun; 300)

Greyfriars Kirk   CHURCH

9 ⊙ MAP P50, D5

One of Edinburgh's most famous churches, Greyfriars Kirk was built on the site of a Franciscan friary and opened for worship on Christmas Day 1620. Surrounding the church, Greyfriars Kirkyard is one of Edinburgh's most evocative cemeteries. (www.greyfriarskirk.com; Greyfriars Pl; 10.30am-4.30pm Mon-Fri, 11am-2pm Sat Apr-Oct, 11am-3pm Thu Nov-Mar; 2, 23, 27, 41, 42, 67)

Greyfriars Kirkyard   CEMETERY

10 ◉ MAP P50, C5

Greyfriars Kirkyard is one of Edinburgh's most evocative cemeteries, a peaceful green oasis dotted with elaborate monuments. Many famous Edinburgh names are buried here, including poet Allan Ramsay (1686–1758); architect William Adam (1689–1748); and William Smellie (1740–95), editor of the first edition of the *Encyclopaedia Britannica*. If you want to experience the graveyard at its scariest – inside a burial vault, in the dark, at night – go on a City of the Dead guided tour. (www.greyfriarskirk.com; Candlemaker Row; ⏲24hr; 🚌2, 23, 27, 41, 42, 67)

Greyfriars Bobby Statue   MONUMENT

11 ◉ MAP P50, D5

Probably the most popular photo opportunity in Edinburgh, the life-size statue of Greyfriars Bobby, a Skye terrier who captured the hearts of the British public in the late 19th century, stands outside Greyfriars Kirkyard. From 1858 to 1872 the wee dog maintained a vigil over the grave of his master, an Edinburgh police officer. The story was immortalised in a novel by Eleanor Atkinson in 1912, and in 1963 was made into a movie by – who else? – Walt Disney. (cnr George IV Bridge & Candlemaker Row; 🚌23, 27, 41, 42, 45, 67)

The Resurrection Men

Edinburgh has long had a reputation for being at the cutting edge of medical research. In the early 19th century this led to a shortage of cadavers with which the city's anatomists could satisfy their curiosity, and an illegal trade in dead bodies emerged.

The readiest supply of corpses was to be found in the city's graveyards. Grave robbers – known as 'resurrection men' – plundered newly buried coffins and sold the cadavers to the anatomists, who turned a blind eye to the source of their research material.

William Burke and William Hare took the body-snatching business a step further, deciding to create their own supply of fresh cadavers by resorting to murder. Between December 1827 and October 1828 they killed at least 16 people, selling their bodies to the surgeon Robert Knox.

When the law finally caught up with them, Hare testified against Burke, who was hanged outside St Giles Cathedral in January 1829. In an ironic twist, his body was given to the anatomy school for public dissection.

Parliament Hall

Before you visit the Scottish Parliament Building, take a look at the magnificent 17th-century **Parliament Hall** (📞0131-348 5355; 11 Parliament Sq; admission free; ⏱10am-4pm Mon-Fri; 🚌2, 23, 27, 41). Tucked behind St Giles Cathedral, it has an original oak hammer-beam roof, and is where the original Scottish Parliament met before its dissolution in 1707. Now used by lawyers and their clients as a meeting place, it's open to the public. As you enter from Parliament Sq (there's a sign outside saying 'Parliament Hall; Court of Session'), you'll see the reception desk in front of you (through a security barrier); the hall is through the double doors immediately on your right.

Canongate Kirkyard CHURCH

12 ◎ MAP P50, H2

The attractive curved gable of the Canongate Kirk, built in 1688, overlooks a kirkyard that contains the graves of several famous people, including economist Adam Smith, author of *The Wealth of Nations;* Agnes Maclehose (the 'Clarinda' of Robert Burns' love poems); and poet Robert Fergusson (1750–74; there's a statue of him on the street outside the church). An information board just inside the gate lists notable graves and their locations. (www. canongatekirk.org.uk; Canongate; ⏱dawn-dusk; 🚌300)

Dovecot Studios ARTS CENTRE

13 ◎ MAP P50, F4

A world-class tapestry studio and contemporary arts-and-crafts centre housed in what was once Edinburgh's oldest public baths, Dovecot has a remarkable history dating back a century. You can watch the weavers at work from a viewing platform above the workshop. The shop and the cafe, which is run by Leo's Beanery, are excellent, too. (📞0131-550 3660; https://dovecotstudios.com; 10 Infirmary St; admission free; ⏱10.30am-5.30pm Mon-Sat)

City Art Centre GALLERY

14 ◎ MAP P50, E3

This art centre comprises six floors of exhibitions with a variety of themes, including an extensive collection of Scottish art. Fees apply for special exhibitions. (www.edinburghmuseums.org.uk; 2 Market St; admission free; ⏱10am-5pm Wed-Sun; ♿; 🚌6)

Eating

Ondine SEAFOOD £££

15 🍴 MAP P50, D4

Ondine is one of Edinburgh's finest seafood restaurants, with a menu based on sustainably sourced fish. Take a seat at the curved Oyster

Bar and tuck into oysters Kilpatrick, smoked-haddock chowder, lobster thermidor, a roast-shellfish platter or just good old haddock and chips (with minted pea purée). (☎ 0131-226 1888; www.ondine restaurant.co.uk; 2 George IV Bridge; mains £18-38, 2-/3-course lunch £19/24; ⏰ noon-3pm & 5.30-10pm Mon-Sat; 🛜; 🚌 23, 27, 41, 42)

Cannonball Restaurant

SCOTTISH ££

16 ⊗ MAP P50, B4

The historic Cannonball House next to Edinburgh Castle's esplanade has been transformed into a sophisticated restaurant (and whisky bar) where the Contini family work their Italian magic on Scottish classics to produce dishes such as haggis balls with spiced pickled turnip and whisky marmalade, and lobster with wild garlic and lemon butter. (☎ 0131-225 1550; www.contini.com/cannon ball; 356 Castlehill; mains £15-25; ⏰ noon-3pm & 5.30-10pm Tue-Sat; 🛜 🚻; 🚌 23, 27, 41, 42)

Mums

CAFE £

17 ⊗ MAP P50, D5

This nostalgia-fuelled cafe serves up classic British comfort food that wouldn't look out of place on a 1950s menu – bacon and eggs, bangers and mash, shepherd's pie, fish and chips. But there's a twist – the food is all top-quality nosh freshly prepared from local produce. There's also a good selection of bottled craft beers and Scottish-brewed cider. (☎ 0131-260

People's Story (p54)

Old Town
History

Before the founding of the New Town in the 18th century, old Edinburgh was an overcrowded and unsanitary hive of humanity. Constrained between the boggy ground of the Nor' Loch (now drained and occupied by Princes Street Gardens) to the north and the city walls to the south and east, the only way for the town to expand was upwards.

Old Town Tenements

The five- to eight-storey tenements that were raised along the Royal Mile in the 16th and 17th centuries were the skyscrapers of their day, remarked upon with wonder by visiting writers such as Daniel Defoe. All classes of society, from beggars to magistrates, lived cheek by jowl in these urban ants nests, the wealthy occupying the middle floors – high enough to be above the noise and stink of the streets, but not so high that climbing the stairs would be too tiring – while the poor squeezed into attics, basements, cellars and vaults.

Royal Mile

The Royal Mile, Edinburgh's oldest street, connects the castle to the Palace of Holyroodhouse. It is split into four named sections: Castlehill, the Lawnmarket, the High St and the Canongate.

A corruption of 'Landmarket', **Lawnmarket** takes its name from a large cloth market (selling goods from the land outside the city) that flourished here until the 18th century; this was the poshest part of the Old Town, where many distinguished citizens made their homes.

High Street, which stretches from George IV Bridge down to St Mary's St, is the heart and soul of the Old Town, home to the city's main church, the law courts, the city chambers and – until 1707 – the Scottish Parliament. The Old Town's eastern gate, the Netherbow Port (part of the Flodden Wall), once stood at the Mary's St end. Though it no longer exists, its former outline is marked by brass strips set in the road.

Canongate – the section between the Netherbow and Holyrood – takes its name from the Augustinian canons (monks) of Holyrood Abbey. From the 16th century it was home to aristocrats who wanted to live near the Palace of Holyroodhouse.

9806; www.monstermashcafe.co.uk; 4a Forrest Rd; mains £9-12; ⏰9am-10pm Mon-Sat, 10am-10pm Sun; 📶♿; 🚌2, 23, 27, 41, 42, 300)

White Horse Oyster & Seafood Bar

SEAFOOD £££

18 ❌ MAP P50, G3

One of Edinburgh's oldest pubs was transformed in 2017 into this intriguing seafood restaurant. The decor is bare stone and wood-panelling in shades of slate grey and brown, providing a dark canvas on which white platters of colourful shellfish and crustaceans shine all the more brightly. The menu also includes small plates (£8 to £12) to accompany a glass of wine. (📞0131-629 5300; www.whitehorseoysterbar.co.uk; 266 Canongate; mains £16-29; ⏰noon-10pm; 🚌6, 300)

Wedgwood

SCOTTISH £££

19 ❌ MAP P50, G3

Fine food without the fuss is the motto at this friendly, unpretentious restaurant. Scottish produce is served with inventive flair in dishes such as beef tartare with soy, shaved egg, scurvy grass and bone-marrow crumb, or spiced monkfish with charred aubergine, pickled chilli and preserved lemon; the menu includes foraged wild salad leaves collected by the chef. (📞0131-558 8737; www.wedgwoodtherestaurant.co.uk; 267 Canongate; mains £18-28, 2-/3-course lunch £16/20; ⏰noon-3pm & 6-10pm; 🚌35)

Tower

SCOTTISH £££

20 ❌ MAP P50, D5

Chic and sleek, with a great view of the castle, Tower is perched in a turret atop the National Museum of Scotland (p42) building. A star-studded guest list of celebrities has enjoyed its menu of quality Scottish food, simply prepared – try half a dozen oysters followed by a 28-day salt-aged rib-eye steak. Afternoon tea (£26) is served from 2pm to 6pm. (📞0131-225 3003; www.tower-restaurant.com; National Museum of Scotland, Chambers St; mains £22-34, 2-course lunch & pre-theatre menu £20; ⏰10am-10pm Sun-Thu, to 10.30pm Fri & Sat; 🚌45, 300)

Witchery by the Castle

SCOTTISH, FRENCH £££

21 ❌ MAP P50, C4

Set in a merchant's townhouse dating from 1595, the Witchery is a candlelit corner of antique splendour with oak-panelled walls, low ceilings, opulent wall hangings and red-leather upholstery; stairs lead down to a second, even more romantic, dining room called the Secret Garden. The menu ranges from oysters to Aberdeen Angus steak and the wine list runs to almost 1000 bins. (📞0131-225 5613; www.thewitchery.com; Castlehill; mains £23-43, 2-course lunch £22; ⏰noon-11.30pm; 🚌23, 27, 41, 42)

Underground Edinburgh

As Edinburgh expanded in the late 18th and early 19th centuries, new bridges were built to link the Old Town to newly developed areas to its north and south. **South Bridge** (completed 1788) and **George IV Bridge** (1834) lead southward from the Royal Mile over the deep valley of the Cowgate, but since their construction so many buildings have clustered around them that you can hardly tell they are bridges. George IV Bridge has a total of nine arches but only two are visible, and South Bridge has no less than 18 hidden arches.

These underground vaults were originally used as storerooms, workshops and drinking dens. But as early 19th-century Edinburgh's population swelled with an influx of penniless Highlanders cleared from their lands, and Irish refugees from the potato famine, the dark, dripping chambers were given over to slum accommodation. The vaults were eventually cleared in the late 19th century, then lay forgotten until 1994 when some of the South Bridge vaults were opened to guided tours (from Mercat Tours; p24), while others are now home to atmospheric nightclubs such as Cabaret Voltaire (p62) and the Caves (p65).

Scott's Kitchen

SCOTTISH, CAFE **£**

22 MAP P50, C4

Green tile, brown leather and arched Georgian windows lend an elegant feel to this modern cafe, which combines fine Scottish produce with great value. Fill up on a breakfast (served till 11.45am) of eggs Benedict, bacon baps or porridge with honey, banana and almonds, or linger over a lunch of Cullen skink, venison casserole, or haggis. (0131-322 6868; https://scottskitchen.co.uk; 4-6 Victoria Tce; mains £8-10; 9am-6pm; P ; 23, 27, 41, 42, 67)

David Bann

VEGETARIAN **££**

23 MAP P50, G3

If you want to convince a carnivorous friend that cuisine à la veg can be as tasty and inventive as a meat-muncher's menu, take them to David Bann's stylish restaurant – dishes such as Puy lentil shepherd's pie, and risotto of braised leek and roasted red pepper are guaranteed to win converts. (0131-556 5888; www.davidbann.com; 56-58 St Mary's St; mains £12-14; noon-10pm Mon-Fri, 11am-10pm Sat & Sun; ; 300)

Amber

SCOTTISH ££

You've got to love a place where the waiter greets you with the words, 'I'll be your whisky adviser for this evening'. Located in the Scotch Whisky Experience (see 3  Map p50, B4) this whisky-themed restaurant manages to avoid the tourist clichés and creates genuinely interesting and flavoursome dishes using top Scottish produce, with a suggested whisky pairing for each dish. (📞0131-477 8477; www.scotchwhiskyexperience.co.uk/restaurant; 354 Castlehill; mains £12-25; ⏰noon-8.30pm Sun-Thu, to 9pm Fri & Sat; 📶👶; 🚌23, 27, 41, 42)

Wings

FAST FOOD £

24 ❌ MAP P50, E4

Eateries don't come much simpler. Order some bowls of barbecued chicken wings (six wings per portion) with the sauce of your choice (there are a couple of dozen to choose from, ranging from tequila and lime juice to hot chilli) and a drink. If you're still hungry, order more. Genius. Great sci-fi/comic-book decor, too. (📞0131-629 1234; www.wingsedinburgh.com; 5/7 Old Fishmarket Close; per portion £3.50; ⏰4-11pm Mon, noon-11pm Tue-Sun; 🚌23, 27, 41, 42)

Scotch Whisky Experience (p52)

Maxie's Bistro

BISTRO ££

25 MAP P50, C4

This candlelit bistro, with its cushion-lined nooks set amid stone walls and wooden beams, is a pleasant setting for a cosy dinner, but at summer lunchtimes people queue for the tables on the terrace overlooking Victoria St. The food is dependable, ranging from pasta, steak and stir-fries to seafood platters and daily specials. Best to book, especially in summer. (📞0131-226 7770; www.maxiesbistro.com; 5b Johnston Tce; mains £11-25; ⏰noon-11pm; 🛜👶; 🚌23, 27, 41, 42)

Drinking

Bow Bar

PUB

26 🍺 MAP P50, C4

One of the city's best traditional-style pubs (it's not as old as it looks), serving a range of excellent real ales, Scottish craft gins and a vast selection of malt whiskies, the Bow Bar often has standing-room only on Friday and Saturday evenings. (www.thebowbar.co.uk; 80 West Bow; ⏰noon-midnight Mon-Sat, to 11.30pm Sun; 🚌2, 23, 27, 41, 42)

Cabaret Voltaire

CLUB

27 🍺 MAP P50, E4

An atmospheric warren of stone-lined vaults houses this self-consciously 'alternative' club, which eschews huge dance floors and egotistical DJ worship in favour of a 'creative crucible'

Sandy Bell's

Sandy Bell's (www.sandybells edinburgh.co.uk; 25 Forrest Rd; ⏰noon-1am Mon-Sat, 12.30pm-midnight Sun; 🚌2, 23, 27, 41, 42, 45) is an unassuming pub that has been a stalwart of the traditional-music scene since the 1960s (the founder's wife sang with the Corries). There's music every weekday evening at 9pm, and from 2pm Saturday and 4pm Sunday, plus lots of impromptu sessions.

hosting an eclectic mix of DJs, live acts, comedy, theatre, visual arts and the spoken word. Well worth a look. (www.thecabaretvoltaire.com; 36-38 Blair St; ⏰5pm-3am Tue-Sat, 8pm-1am Sun; 🛜; 🚌all South Bridge buses)

Bongo Club

CLUB

28 🍺 MAP P50, D4

Owned by a local arts charity, the weird and wonderful Bongo Club boasts a long history of hosting everything from wild club nights and local bands to performance art and kids comedy shows. (www.thebongoclub.co.uk; 66 Cowgate; free-£7; ⏰11pm-3am Tue & Thu, 7pm-3am Fri-Sun; 🛜; 🚌2)

BrewDog

BAR

29 🍺 MAP P50, E4

The Edinburgh outpost of Scotland's self-styled 'punk brewery',

BrewDog stands out among the sticky-floored dives that line the Cowgate, with its polished-concrete bar and cool, industrial-chic decor. As well as its own highly rated beers, there's a choice of guest real ales, and – a sign of a great trad pub – coat hooks under the edge of the bar. (www.brewdog.com; 143 Cowgate; ☺noon-1am; 🛜; 🚍45, 300)

Salt Horse Beer Shop & Bar
BAR

30 🚍 MAP P50, F4

Tucked off the Royal Mile, this independent hybrid combines great beer, food, and a shop next door selling around 400 beers to drink in or take away. Work your way through 12 keg lines of local and imported beers and a small but perfectly formed menu of handmade burgers, Scotch eggs, and charcuterie and cheese platters. (📞0131-558 8304; www.salthorse.beer; 57-61 Blackfriars St; ☺4pm-midnight Mon-Fri, noon-1am Sat, 12.30pm-midnight Sun; 🚍300)

Checkpoint
BAR

31 🚍 MAP P50, E5

A friendly cafe, bar and restaurant with a comprehensive menu including breakfasts, bar bites and substantial mains, Checkpoint is gaining a reputation as one of the coolest spots in Edinburgh. The utilitarian white-walled space is flooded with light from floor-to-ceiling windows and is vast enough to house, of all things, an old shipping container. (📞0131-225 9352;

Bow Bar

Music at St Giles

St Giles Cathedral (www.st gilescathedral.org.uk; High St; 23, 27, 41, 42) plays host to a regular and varied program of classical music, including popular lunchtime and evening concerts and organ recitals. The cathedral choir sings at the 10am and 11.30am Sunday services.

www.checkpointedinburgh.com; 3 Bristo Pl; ⊘9am-1am; 🔊; 🚊2, 47)

Paradise Palms BAR

32 📍 MAP P50, E5

If you like your student bars grungy and unpretentious, with affordable left-field cocktails (Buckfast Daiquiri, anyone?), delicious vegetarian soul food and banging music, Paradise Palms is for you. There's lots of neon, disco balls and stuffed toys hanging above the bar. Regular DJ and cabaret nights. (☏0131-225 4186; www.theparadise palms.com; 41 Lothian St; ⊘noon-1am; ; 🚊2, 41, 42, 47, 67)

Holyrood 9A PUB

33 📍 MAP P50, G4

Candlelight flickering off hectares of polished wood creates an atmospheric setting for this superb real-ale bar, with more than 20 taps pouring craft beers from all corners of the country and indeed the globe. If you're peckish, it serves excellent gourmet burgers, too. (www.theholyrood.co.uk; 9a Holyrood Rd; ⊘9am-midnight Sun-Thu to 1am Fri & Sat; 🔊; 🚊36)

Liquid Room CLUB

34 📍 MAP P50, C4

Set in a subterranean vault deep beneath Victoria St, the Liquid Room is a superb club venue with a thundering sound system. There are regular club nights every Friday and Saturday, as well as DJs and live bands on other nights. Check website for upcoming events. (www.liquidroom.com; 9c Victoria St; free-£20; ⊘live music from 7pm, club nights 10.30pm-3am; 🚊23, 27, 41, 42)

Jolly Judge PUB

35 📍 MAP P50, C3

A snug little howff tucked away down a close, the Judge exudes a cosy 17th-century atmosphere (low, timber-beamed painted ceilings) and has the added attraction of a cheering open fire in cold weather. No music or gaming machines, just the buzz of conversation. (www.jollyjudge.co.uk; 7a James Ct; ⊘noon-11pm Mon-Thu, to midnight Fri & Sat, 12.30-11pm Sun; 🔊; 🚊23, 27, 41, 42)

Malt Shovel PUB

36 📍 MAP P50, D3

A traditional-looking pub with dark wood and subdued tartanry, the Malt Shovel offers a good range of real ales and more than 40 malt whiskies, and serves excellent pub grub including fish and chips, burgers, and steak-and-ale pies. (☎ 0131-225 6843; www.maltshovelinn-edinburgh.co.uk; 11-15 Cockburn St; ⏰ 11am-11pm Mon-Wed, to midnight Thu & Sun, to 1am Fri & Sat; 📶 🚻; 🚌 6)

Entertainment

Caves LIVE MUSIC

37 ⭐ MAP P50, F4

A spectacular subterranean venue set in the ancient stone vaults beneath the South Bridge, the Caves stages a series of one-off club nights and live-music gigs, as well as *ceilidh* (traditional music) nights during the Edinburgh Festival. Check the What's On link on the website for upcoming events. (https://unusualvenues edinburgh.com/venues/the-caves-venue-edinburgh; 8-12 Niddry St S; 🚌 300)

Royal Oak TRADITIONAL MUSIC

38 ⭐ MAP P50, F4

This popular folk-music pub is tiny, so get here early (9pm start weekdays, 6pm and 9.30pm sessions on Saturday, 4.30pm and 7pm sessions on Sunday) if you want to be sure of a place. Saturday night in the lounge is open session – bring your own instrument (and/or a good singing voice!). (www.royal-oak-folk.com; 1 Infirmary St; ⏰ 11.30am-2am Mon-Sat, 12.30pm-2am Sun; 🚌 all South Bridge buses)

Traveller performing at The Caves

The Scotsman Steps

This is public art at its best: harmonious, understated and accessible. In 2010 Turner Prize winner Martin Creed was commissioned by the **Fruitmarket Gallery** (www.fruitmarket.co.uk; 45 Market St; admission free; ⏰11am-6pm; ♿; 🚌6) to create a permanent work for Edinburgh's historic **Scotsman Steps** (www.fruitmarket.co.uk/scotsman-steps; admission free; 🚌6, all North Bridge buses), built in 1899 to link the Old and New Towns. Using 104 different-coloured marbles for each of the 104 steps, this elegant work has revitalised a neglected corner of the city. There are entrances on Market St and North Bridge.

Jazz Bar
JAZZ, BLUES

39 ⭐ MAP P50, F4

This atmospheric cellar bar, with its polished parquet floors, bare stone walls, candlelit tables and stylish steel-framed chairs, is owned and operated by jazz musicians. There's live music every night from 9pm to 3am, and on Saturday from 3pm; as well as jazz, expect bands playing blues, funk, soul and fusion. (www.thejazzbar.co.uk; 1a Chambers St; £3-7; ⏰5pm-3am Sun-Fri, 1.30pm-3am Sat; 🔊; 🚌45, 300)

Bannerman's
LIVE MUSIC

40 ⭐ MAP P50, F4

A long-established music venue – it seems like every Edinburgh student for the last four decades spent half their youth here – Bannerman's straggles through a warren of old vaults beneath South Bridge. It pulls in crowds of students, locals and backpackers with live rock, punk and indie bands five or six nights a week. (www.facebook.com/BannermansBar; 212 Cowgate; ⏰noon-1am Mon-Sat, 12.30pm-1am Sun; 🔊; 🚌45, 300)

Whistle Binkie's
LIVE MUSIC

41 ⭐ MAP P50, F3

This crowded cellar bar, just off the Royal Mile, has live music most nights till 3am, from rock and blues to folk and jazz. The long-standing open-mic night on Monday is a showcase for new talent. (www.whistlebinkies.com; 4-6 South Bridge; admission free, except after midnight Fri & Sat; ⏰5pm-3am Sun-Thu, 1pm-3am Fri & Sat; 🚌all South Bridge buses)

Bedlam Theatre
COMEDY

42 ⭐ MAP P50, D5

The Bedlam hosts a long-established (running for more than 25 years) weekly improvisation slot, the Improverts, which is hugely popular with local students. Shows kick off at 10.30pm every Friday during term time, and you're guaranteed a robust and entertaining evening. (📞0131-629 0430; www.bedlamtheatre.co.uk; 11b Bristo Pl; £3.50; 🚌2, 23, 27, 41, 42)

Shopping

Armstrong's   VINTAGE

43 🔒 MAP P50, C5

Armstrong's is an Edinburgh fashion institution (established in 1840, no less), a quality vintage-clothes emporium offering everything from elegant 1940s dresses to funky 1970s flares. Aside from the retro fashion, it's a great place to hunt for pre-loved kilts and Harris tweed, or to seek inspiration for that fancy-dress party. (📞0131-220 5557; www.armstrongsvintage.co.uk; 83 Grassmarket; ⏰10am-5.30pm Mon-Thu, to 6pm Fri & Sat, noon-6pm Sun; 🚌2)

Royal Mile Whiskies   DRINKS

44 🔒 MAP P50, D3

If it's a drap of the cratur ye're after, this place has a selection of single malts in miniature and full-size bottles. There's also a range of blended whiskies, Irish whiskey and bourbon, and you can buy online, too. (📞0131-225 3383; www.royalmilewhiskies.com; 379 High St; ⏰10am-7pm Sun-Wed, to 8pm Thu-Sat; 🚌23, 27, 41, 42)

Bill Baber   FASHION & ACCESSORIES

45 🔒 MAP P50, C4

This family-run designer-knitwear studio has been in the business for more than 30 years, producing stylish and colourful creations using linen, merino wool, silk and cotton. (📞0131-225 3249; www.

Armstrong's vintage shop

billbaber.com; 66 Grassmarket; 9am-5.30pm Mon-Sat, 11am-4pm Sun; 2)

Hannah Zakari
JEWELLERY

46 MAP P50, D4

This is Edinburgh's coolest jewellery boutique, sourcing quirky pieces by indie designers from all over the world. Necklaces, earrings, brooches, cards, art prints and accessories are gorgeously presented in a small shop that has been hit-listed in *Vogue*, *Tatler* and the *Guardian*. Pleasing to the eye, dangerous for the wallet. (0131-226 5433; www.hannahzakari.co.uk; 43 Candlemaker Row; noon-5.30pm Mon-Fri, 11am-5.30pm Sat, 12.30pm-4.30pm Sun; 2, 23, 27, 41, 42, 45)

Ragamuffin
FASHION & ACCESSORIES

47 MAP P50, G3

Quality Scottish knitwear and fabrics, including cashmere from Johnstons of Elgin, Fair Isle sweaters and Harris tweed. (0131-557 6007; www.facebook.com/pg/ragamuffinclothesandknitwear; 278 Canongate; 10am-6pm Mon-Sat, noon-6pm Sun; 35)

Godiva
FASHION & ACCESSORIES

48 MAP P50, B5

This unconventional, innovative boutique specialises in both vintage and modern, cutting-edge designs. It has been awarded accolades in the Scottish Variety Awards, and is committed to ethical fashion. (0131-221 9212; www.godivaboutique.co.uk; 9 West Port;

10.30am-5.30pm Mon-Fri, 10am-6pm Sat, 11.30am-5.30pm Sun; 2)

Geoffrey (Tailor) Inc
FASHION & ACCESSORIES

49 MAP P50, F3

Geoffrey can fit you out in traditional Highland dress, or run up a kilt in your own clan tartan. The store's offshoot, 21st Century Kilts (p93), offers modern fashion kilts in a variety of fabrics. (0131-557 0256; www.geoffreykilts.co.uk; 57-59 High St; 9.30am-6pm Mon-Sat, 10.30am-5.30pm Sun; 300)

Blackwell's Bookshop
BOOKS

50 MAP P50, F4

The city's principal bookstore, covering all subjects; it has a huge selection of academic books. (0131-622 8222; www.blackwell.co.uk; 53-62 South Bridge; 9am-8pm Mon, Tue, Thu & Fri, 9.30am-8pm Wed, 9am-6pm Sat, noon-6pm Sun; all South Bridge buses)

Joyce Forsyth Designer Knitwear
FASHION & ACCESSORIES

51 MAP P50, D5

The colourful knitwear on show at this intriguing little shop will drag your ideas about woollens firmly into the 21st century. Ms Forsyth's trademark design is a flamboyant, flared woollen coat (it can be knitted to order in colours of your choice), but there are also box jackets, jumpers, hats, scarves and shawls. (0131-220 4112; www.joyceforsyth.co.uk; 42 Candlemaker

Cockburn St Shops

Cockburn St is packed with trendy shops and boutiques where Edinburgh teens and 20-somethings flock to browse the fashion rails. Look out for these highlights.

Pie in the Sky (0131-220 1477; www.facebook.com/pieinthesky72; 47 Cockburn St; 10am-6pm; 6) Vintage and alternative fashion.

Underground Solush'n (0131-226 2242; www.undergroundsolushn. com; 9 Cockburn St; 10am-6pm Mon-Wed, Fri & Sat, 10am-7pm Thu, noon-6pm Sun; 6) New and secondhand vinyl; one of the city's best record shops.

Cookie (0131-622 7260; www.facebook.com/cookiecockburnstreet; 29a Cockburn St; 10am-6pm; 6) Cute party dresses.

Museum Context (0131-629 0534; www.facebook.com/museum contextuk; 42-44 Cockburn St; 10am-6pm Mon-Sat, 11am-5pm Sun; 6) Aladdin's cave of unusual gifts.

Row; 10am-5.30pm Tue-Sat; 2, 23, 27, 41, 42, 45)

Mr Wood's Fossils

GIFTS & SOUVENIRS

52 MAP P50, C4

Founded by famous fossil hunter Stan Wood, who discovered 'Lizzie', the oldest fossil reptile yet known, this fascinating speciality shop has a wide range of minerals, gems, fossils and other geological gifts. (0131-220 1344; www.mrwoods fossils.co.uk; 5 Cowgatehead; 10am-5.30pm; 2)

Kilberry Bagpipes

MUSICAL INSTRUMENTS

53 MAP P50, G3

A maker and retailer of traditional Highland bagpipes, Kilberry also sells piping accessories, snare drums, books, CDs and learning materials. (0131-556 9607; www. kilberrybagpipes.com; 27 St Mary's St; 8.30am-4.30pm Mon-Fri, 10am-2pm Sat; 6, 300)

Explore ◈
Holyrood & Arthur's Seat

Facing the imposing royal Palace of Holyroodhouse at the foot of the Royal Mile, a once near-derelict district has been transformed by the construction of the Scottish Parliament Building. Holyrood Park, a former hunting ground of Scottish monarchs centred on the miniature mountain of Arthur's Seat, allows Edinburghers to enjoy a little bit of wilderness in the heart of the city.

The Palace of Holyroodhouse (p72) can get very busy during the main part of the day – get there first thing in the morning to avoid the worst of the crowds, and allow two hours to explore it and neighbouring 12th-century Holyrood Abbey (p73). Break for lunch at Kilderkin (p82) or Hemma (p82), then set aside an hour each for the Scottish Parliament Building (p74) and Our Dynamic Earth (p80). Climb to the summit of Arthur's Seat (p79) to enjoy the early evening view and to work up an appetite for a sumptuous, over-the-top dinner at Rhubarb (p81).

Getting There & Around

🚌 Lothian Bus services 6 and 300 both run to Holyrood, 300 (from the airport) via the lower half of the Royal Mile and 6 via Holyrood Rd. Bus 42 runs along Duddingston Rd West, a short walk from Duddingston Village, while 4, 5, 15, 26, 44 and 45 run along London Rd, near the north entrance to Holyrood Park.

Neighbourhood Map on p78

Palace of Holyroodhouse (p72) HARALD LUEDER/SHUTTERSTOCK ©

Top Sight 📷
Palace of Holyroodhouse

The Palace of Holyroodhouse is the royal family's official residence in Scotland, but it is probably most famous as the home of the ill-fated Mary, Queen of Scots. She spent six turbulent years here from 1561 to 1567, during which time she debated with John Knox, married her second and third husbands, and witnessed the murder of her secretary David Rizzio.

◎ MAP P78, B2

www.royalcollection.
org.uk/visit/palace-of-
holyroodhouse

Canongate, Royal Mile

adult/child incl audioguide
£14/8.10

🕐 9.30am-6pm, last
entry 4.30pm Apr-Oct, to
4.30pm, last entry 3.15pm
Nov-Mar

🚌 6, 300

Great Gallery

A self-guided audio tour leads you through a series of impressive royal apartments, ending in the Great Gallery. The 89 portraits of Scottish kings (both real and legendary) were commissioned by Charles II and supposedly record his unbroken lineage from Scota, the Egyptian pharaoh's daughter who discovered the infant Moses in a reed basket on the banks of the Nile.

Mary's Bedchamber

The highlight of the tour is a bedchamber that was home to the unfortunate Mary, Queen of Scots, from 1561 to 1567 (it's connected to her husband's bedchamber by a **secret stairway**). It was here that her jealous second husband, Lord Darnley, restrained the pregnant queen while his henchmen murdered her secretary – and favourite – David Rizzio; a plaque in the neighbouring room marks the spot where he bled to death.

Holyrood Abbey

Admission to the palace includes a guided tour of neighbouring **Holyrood Abbey** (pictured left; www.historicenvironment.scot/visit-a-place/places/holyrood-abbey; Canongate; with Palace of Holyroodhouse free; ⏰9.30am-6pm, last entry 4.30pm Apr-Oct, to 4.30pm, last entry 3.15pm Nov-Mar; 🚌6, 300), founded by David I in 1128. It was probably named after a fragment of the True Cross, on which Christ was crucified (*rood* is an old Scots word for cross), said to have been brought back from the Holy Land by his mother, St Margaret. Most of the surviving ruins date from the 12th and 13th centuries; the royal burial vault holds the remains of David II, James II and James V, and Lord Darnley, husband of of Mary, Queen of Scots.

★ Top Tips

o The palace is closed to the public when the royal family is visiting and during state functions (usually in mid-May, and mid-June to early July); check the website for exact dates.

o You can wander through the palace at your own speed; an audioguide is included in the price of admission. Allow at least one to 1½ hours.

o If you plan to visit the Queen's Gallery (p80) as well, you can buy a combined ticket.

✕ Take a Break

The **Café at the Palace** (Mews Courtyard, Queen's Gallery, Horse Wynd; mains £6-10; ⏰9.30am-6pm Apr-Oct, to 4.30pm Nov-Mar; 🚌6, 300), in the courtyard of the Queen's Gallery, serves soup and snacks.

Hemma (p82) is a short walk away, and does family-friendly food.

Top Sight 📷
Scottish Parliament Building

The Scottish Parliament Building is a spectacular example of modern architecture, designed by Catalan architect Enric Miralles and officially opened by the Queen in 2004. It's an original and idiosyncratic building that caused a great deal of controversy at the time but now provides a home for the parliament created in the wake of the Scottish devolution referendum of 1997.

◎ MAP P78, B2

www.parliament.scot

Horse Wynd

admission free

🕙 9am-6.30pm Tue-Thu, 10am-5pm Mon, Fri & Sat in session, 10am-5pm Tue-Thu in recess

🚌 6, 300

The Exterior

Architect Enric Miralles (1955–2000) believed that a building could be a work of art. However, this weird concrete confection has left many people scratching their heads in confusion. What does it all mean? The strange forms of the exterior are each symbolic in some way, from the oddly shaped projecting windows on the western wall (inspired by the silhouette of *The Reverend Robert Walker Skating on Duddingston Loch,* one of Scotland's most famous paintings) to the unusual, inverted-L-shaped panels on the facade (representing a curtain being drawn aside, ie open government). The ground plan of the whole complex represents a 'flower of democracy rooted in Scottish soil' (best seen looking down from Salisbury Crags).

The Debating Chamber

The **Main Hall**, inside the public entrance, has a low, triple-arched ceiling of polished concrete, like a cave, or cellar, or castle vault. It is a dimly lit space, the starting point for a metaphorical journey from this relative darkness up to the Debating Chamber (sitting directly above the Main Hall), which is, in contrast, a palace of light – the light of democracy. This magnificent chamber is the centrepiece of the parliament, designed not to glorify but to humble the politicians who sit within it. The windows face Calton Hill, allowing members of the Scottish parliament (MSPs) to look up to its monuments (reminders of the Scottish Enlightenment), while the massive, pointed oak beams of the roof are suspended by steel threads above the MSPs' heads like so many Damoclean swords.

★ Top Tips

o The public areas of the parliament building – the Main Hall, where there is an exhibition, a shop and cafe, and the public gallery in the Debating Chamber – are open to visitors. Tickets are needed for the public gallery – see the website for details.

o You can also take a free, one-hour guided tour (advance bookings recommended).

o If you want to see the parliament in session, check the website for sitting times – business days are normally Tuesday to Thursday year-round.

✕ Take a Break

There is a cafe in the Parliament Building at the rear of the Main Hall, and another across the street in the Queen's Gallery.

Walking Tour 🥾

A Walk Through Holyrood Park

Holyrood Park covers 650 acres of varied land-scape, including crags, moorland and lochs, plus the miniature mountain of Arthur's Seat, little changed since its enclosure as a royal hunting ground in the 16th century. It's a wildlife haven and a huge recreational resource for the city, thronged with walkers, cyclists and picnickers on sunny weekends.

Walk Facts

Start Holyrood Park, northern entrance

End Duddingston Village

Length 2.6 miles; 2 hours

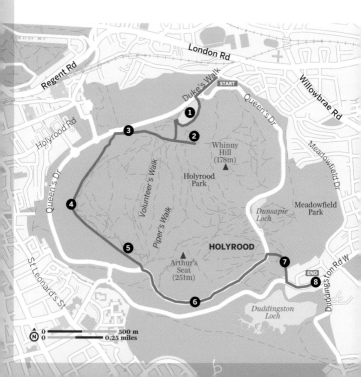

❶ St Margaret's Loch

Begin at the park's northern entrance on Duke's Walk, which leads to St Margaret's Loch, an artificial pond created during Victorian times. The loch is well known for its huge flocks of swans and ducks (please don't feed them – human food is not healthy for wild animals).

❷ St Anthony's Chapel

Take the path on the south side of the loch and climb up to the ruins of St Anthony's Chapel. Dating from the 15th century, its origins are obscure; it may have been associated with a hospital in Leith donated by King James I (for the treatment of the skin disease erysipelas, also known as St Anthony's Fire), or it may have been a beacon for ships in the Firth of Forth.

❸ St Margaret's Well

Descend back to the road where you'll find St Margaret's Well, a beautiful, late-15th-century Gothic well-house. It was moved, stone by stone, to this location in 1860 when its original site in Meadowbank was taken over by a railway depot. You can't get into the chamber – all you can do is peek at the ornate vaulting through the metal grille at the entrance.

❹ Radical Road

The park's most dramatic feature is the long, curving sweep of Salisbury Crags, a russet curtain of columnar basaltic cliffs. The stony path along the foot of the crags is known as the Radical Road – it was built in 1820, at the suggestion of Sir Walter Scott, to give work to unemployed weavers (from whose politics it took its name).

❺ Hutton's Section

At the southern end of the crags, look out for an interpretation board set in a boulder marking Hutton's Section. Edinburgh's most famous rock outcrop was used by the pioneering geologist James Hutton in 1788 to bolster his theory that the basaltic rocks of Salisbury Crags were formed by the cooling of molten lava.

❻ Queen's Drive

Continue onto Queen's Dr, built in the 19th century as a scenic carriage drive for Queen Victoria and Prince Albert during their stays at Holyroodhouse. Closed to motor vehicles on Sundays, the drive winds across the southern slopes of Arthur's Seat, with grand views over the city to the Pentland Hills.

❼ Jacob's Ladder

Where the road curves sharply to the north (left), a (signposted) footpath on the right leads to Jacob's Ladder, a steep staircase of 209 steps that descends the western edge of Duddingston Village.

❽ Duddingston Village

The picturesque little village of Duddingston dates from the 12th century, though only the church survives from that era; most of the houses were built in the 18th century, including the village pub, the **Sheep Heid Inn** (p82), a good place to stop for lunch or a pint.

A — London Rd — B

Royal Terrace Gardens

Royal Tce

1 Calton Hill

Regent Gardens

C

D

London Rd

Regent Rd

⊙13

Montrose Tce

Atholhill

Burns Monument **⊙8** Calton New Burial Ground

Queen's Gallery

2 Calton Rd

⊙12

⊙5

⊙ Palace of Holyroodhouse

St Margaret Loch

Canongate (Royal Mile)

⊙7

⊙ Scottish Parliament Building

Scottish Poetry Library

⊙10

⊙4

Our Dynamic Earth

Queen's Dr

3 Holyrood Rd

⊙14

The Pleasance

Queen's Dr

Volunteer's Walk

Piper's Walk

3

Holyrood Park

Radical Rd

Arthur's Seat **⊙1**

4

▲ Arthur Seat (251m)

St Leonard's St

5

Dalkeith Rd

Holyrood Park Rd

Queen's Dr

S Clerk St

6 E Preston St

University of Edinburgh Pollock Halls of Residence

2⊙
6⊙
11⊙

⊗9

Prestonfield Golf Course

N
0 ——— 500 m
0 ——— 0.25 miles

A — B — C — D

For reviews see	
⊙ Top Sights	p72
⊙ Sights	p79
⊗ Eating	p81
⊖ Drinking	p82
✩ Entertainment	p83

Sights

Arthur's Seat

VIEWPOINT

1 MAP P78, D5

The rocky peak of Arthur's Seat (251m), carved by ice sheets from the deeply eroded stump of a long-extinct volcano, is a distinctive feature of Edinburgh's skyline. The view from the summit is well worth the walk, extending from the Forth bridges in the west to the distant conical hill of North Berwick Law in the east, with the Ochil Hills and the Highlands on the northwestern horizon. You can hike from Holyrood to the summit in around 45 minutes. (Holyrood Park; 🚌 6, 300)

Dr Neil's Garden

GARDENS

2 ⊙ MAP P78, D6

Edinburgh's quintessential secret garden, in the shadow of a 12th-century kirk, is one of the most peaceful green spaces in Scotland. Cultivated in the 1960s by doctors Andrew and Nancy Neil from a scrappy piece of wilderness where Arthur's Seat slopes down to Duddingston Loch, the planting is a mixture of conifers, heathers and alpines, with a remarkable physic garden. Seek out a bench and soak up the meditative atmosphere of this special place. (📞 07849 187995; www.drneilsgarden.co.uk; Old Church Lane, Duddingston Village; admission free; ⊙10am-dusk; 🚌42)

Arthur's Seat

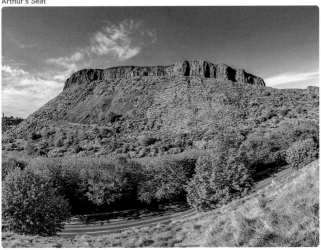

Holyrood & Arthur's Seat Sights

Urban Hillwalking on Arthur's Seat

To climb Arthur's Seat from Holyrood, cross Queen's Dr and follow the path that slants leftward up the hillside from the north end of Salisbury Crags, heading towards the ruins of St Anthony's Chapel, then turn south on a rough path that follows the floor of a shallow dip just east of Long Row crags. The path eventually curves around to the left and rises more steeply up some steps to a saddle; turn right here and climb to the rocky summit of Arthur's Seat.

Holyrood Park PARK

3 ◉ MAP P78, B4

In Holyrood Park Edinburgh is blessed with a little bit of wilderness in the heart of the city. The former hunting ground of Scottish monarchs, the park covers 263 hectares of varied landscape, including crags, moorland and loch, and the 251m summit of Arthur's Seat (p79). Holyrood Park can be circumnavigated by car or bike along Queen's Dr. (🚌6, 300)

Our Dynamic Earth MUSEUM

4 ◉ MAP P78, B3

Housed in a modernistic white marquee, Our Dynamic Earth is an interactive, multimedia journey of discovery through Earth's history from the Big Bang to the present day. Hugely popular with kids of all ages, it's a slick extravaganza of whiz-bang special effects and 3D movies cleverly designed to fire up young minds with curiosity about all things geological and environmental. Its true purpose, of course, is to disgorge you into a gift shop where you can buy toy dinosaurs and souvenir T-shirts. (www.dynamicearth.co.uk; Holyrood Rd; adult/child £15.50/9.75; ⏰10am-5.30pm Easter-Oct, to 6pm Jul & Aug, 10am-5.30pm Wed-Sun Nov-Easter; 🚻; 🚌6, 300)

Queen's Gallery GALLERY

5 ◉ MAP P78, B2

This stunning modern gallery, which occupies the shell of a former church and school, is a showcase for exhibitions of art from the Royal Collections. The exhibitions change every six months or so; for current details, check the website. (www.royalcollection.org.uk/visit/the-queens-gallery-palace-of-holyroodhouse; Horse Wynd; adult/child £7/3.50, with Holyroodhouse £17.50/10; ⏰9.30am-6pm, last entry 4.30pm Apr-Oct, to 4.30pm, last entry 3.15pm Nov-Mar; 🚌6, 300)

Duddingston Kirk CHURCH

6 ◉ MAP P78, D6

Poised on a promontory overlooking Duddingston Loch, this church is one of the oldest buildings in Edinburgh, with some interesting medieval relics at the kirkyard gate: the *joug*, a metal collar that was used, like the stocks, to tether criminals and sinners, and the *loupin-on stane*, a stone step to help gouty and corpulent parishioners get onto their horses. The early 19th-century **watchtower** inside the gate was built to deter body snatchers (p55). (www.duddingstonkirk.co.uk; Old Church Lane, Duddingston Village; admission free; ⊙10am-4pm Thu-Sat, 1-4pm Wed & Sun; ⊟42)

Scottish Poetry Library
MUSEUM

7 ◉ MAP P78, A2

A fantastic literary resource housed in award-winning modern architecture off Canongate, the poetry library hosts regular exhibitions and is a source of information on the mysterious Edinburgh Book Sculptures (p82). (☎0131-557 2876; www.spl.org.uk; 5 Crichton's Cl; admission free; ⊙10am-5pm Tue-Fri, to 4pm Sat; ⊟6, 300)

Burns Monument
MONUMENT

8 ◉ MAP P78, A2

The neoclassical Burns Monument (1830), a Greek-style memorial to Scotland's national poet Robert Burns, stands on the southern flank of Calton Hill. It was designed by Thomas Hamilton, a former pupil of the Royal High School (now closed), which stands just across the road. (Regent Rd; ⊟4, 5, 34)

Eating

Rhubarb
SCOTTISH £££

9 ⊗ MAP P78, C6

Set in the splendid 17th-century **Prestonfield hotel**, Rhubarb is a feast for the eyes as well as the

---

Mystery of the Miniature Coffins

In July 1836 some boys hunting for rabbits on the slopes of Arthur's Seat made a strange discovery: in a hollow beneath a rock, arranged on a pile of slates, were 17 tiny wooden coffins. Each was just four inches (10cm) long and contained a roughly carved human figure dressed in handmade clothes.

Many theories have been put forward in explanation, but the most convincing is that the coffins were made in response to the infamous Burke and Hare murders of 1831–32: the number of coffins matched the number of known victims. It was a common belief that people whose bodies had been dissected by anatomists could not enter heaven, and it is thought that someone fashioned the tiny figures in order to provide the murder victims with a form of Christian burial.

Eight of the 17 coffins survive, and can be seen in the National Museum of Scotland (p42). Edinburgh author Ian Rankin makes use of the story of the coffins in his detective novel *The Falls*.

taste buds. The over-the-top decor of rich reds set off with black and gold and the sensuous surfaces that make you want to touch everything – damask, brocade, marble, gilded leather – are matched by the intense flavours and rich textures of the modern Scottish cuisine. (📞0131-225 1333; www.prestonfield.com/dine/rhubarb; Prestonfield, Priestfield Rd; mains £26-40; ⏰noon-2pm & 6-10pm Mon-Sat, 12.30-3pm & 6-10pm Sun; P)

Drinking

Hemma   BAR

10 🍺 MAP P78, B3

Set among the glass-and-steel architecture of the redeveloped Holyrood district, Hemma (Swedish for 'at home') is one of a stable of Scandinavian bars, a funky fish tank of a place furnished with comfy armchairs and sofas and brightly coloured wooden chairs. Good coffee and cakes during the day; real ale and cocktails in the evening. (📞0131-629 3327; www.

bodabar.com/hemma; 75 Holyrood Rd; ⏰11am-8pm Mon, to 11pm Tue & Wed, to midnight Thu, to 1am Fri & Sat, 10am-8pm Sun; 📶♿; 🚌6, 300)

Sheep Heid Inn   PUB

11 🍺 MAP P78, D6

Possibly the oldest inn in Edinburgh (with a licence dating back to 1360), the Sheep Heid feels more like an upmarket country pub than an Edinburgh bar. Set in the semi-rural shadow of Arthur's Seat (p79), it's famous for its 19th-century skittles alley and its lovely little beer garden. (www.thesheepheid edinburgh.co.uk; 43-45 The Causeway; ⏰11am-11pm Mon-Thu, to midnight Fri & Sat, noon-11pm Sun; ♿; 🚌42)

Kilderkin   PUB

12 🍺 MAP P78, B2

A successful attempt at reinventing the local neighbourhood pub, with polished mahogany, stained glass and snug booths, the Kilderkin stages regular community-building events such as quizzes, open-mic

---

Edinburgh's Mysterious Book Sculptures

In 2011 and 2012 an unknown artist left a series of intricate and beautiful paper sculptures in various Edinburgh libraries, museums and bookshops (more sculptures appeared in 2013 and 2014). Each was fashioned from an old book and alluded to literary themes; a message from the anonymous artist revealed they had been inspired by the poem 'Gifts', by Edinburgh poet Norman MacCaig. Two are on display at the Scottish Poetry Library (p81), where you can pick up a self-guided walking-tour leaflet, *Gifted: The Edinburgh Book Sculptures* (also available on the library's website).

Scottish Poetry Library (p81)

evenings, ukulele nights and whisky-tasting sessions. The bar serves hand-pulled pints of cask ale, more than 100 varieties of rum, and decent food. (📞0131-556 2101; www.kilderkin.co.uk; 67 Canongate; 🕐11am-midnight Mon-Fri, to 1am Sat, 12.30-8pm Sun; 🛜👶; 🚌6, 300)

Regent PUB

13 📍 MAP P78, C1

This is a pleasant gay local with a relaxed atmosphere (no loud music), serving coffee and croissants as well as excellent real ales, including Deuchars IPA and Caledonian 80/-. Meeting place for the Lesbian and Gay Real Ale Drinkers club (first Monday of the month at 9pm). (📞0131-661 8198; 2 Montrose Tce; 🕐noon-1am Mon-Sat, 12.30pm-1am Sun; 🚌1, 4, 5, 15, 45, 300)

Entertainment

Edinburgh Folk Club LIVE MUSIC

14 📍 MAP P78, A3

The Pleasance Theatre Bar is the home venue of the Edinburgh Folk Club, which runs a program of visiting bands and singers at 8pm on Wednesday nights. (www.edinburgh folkclub.co.uk; Pleasance Courtyard, 60 The Pleasance; £12; 🚌6, 14)

Explore ⊛
New Town

Edinburgh's New Town is the world's most complete and unspoilt example of Georgian architecture and town planning; along with the Old Town, it was declared a Unesco World Heritage Site in 1995. Princes St is one of Britain's most spectacular shopping streets, with unbroken views of the castle, while George St is lined with designer boutiques, trendy bars and upmarket restaurants.

A morning stroll along Princes St will reveal the grandeur of Edinburgh's setting. Take in the view from the top of the Scott Monument (p89), and browse the art at the Scottish National Gallery (p96) before a lunch of local cuisine in the Scottish Cafe & Restaurant (p103).

Enjoy an afternoon shopping (p92) in the New Town, and visiting the Scottish National Portrait Gallery (p86). Save a climb up Calton Hill (p97) for the end of the day, as the evening views over the Firth of Forth to the Forth bridges can be stunning. End your day with an indulgent dinner at Contini (p100) or Number One (p101).

Getting There & Around

🚌 Just about every bus service in Edinburgh runs along Princes St at some point in its journey, but note that not all buses stop at every bus stop – if you're looking for a particular bus, check the route numbers listed on the bus-stop sign.

🚊 The tram line runs from the West End along Princes St to York Pl.

Neighbourhood Map on p94

View of Princes Street from Calton Hill (p97) ANDREYSPB21/SHUTTERSTOCK ©

Top Sight 📷
Scottish National Portrait Gallery

The renovated Venetian Gothic palace of the Scottish National Portrait Gallery reopened in 2011, emerging as one of the city's top attractions. Its galleries illustrate Scottish history through paintings, photographs and sculptures, putting faces to Scotland's famous names, from Robert Burns, Mary, Queen of Scots, and Bonnie Prince Charlie to actor Sean Connery, comedian Billy Connolly and poet Jackie Kay.

◎ MAP P94, E3

☏ 0131-624 6200

www.nationalgalleries.org

1 Queen St

admission free

🕙 10am-5pm

♿

🚌 all York Pl buses, 🚇 St Andrew Sq

Architecture

The museum's exterior is a neo-Gothic froth of friezes, pinnacles and sculptures – the niches at 1st-floor level hold statues of Scottish kings and queens, philosophers and poets, artists and scientists. Mary, Queen of Scots, is in the middle of the east wall on North St Andrew St, while the main entrance is framed by Robert the Bruce and William Wallace.

Great Hall

The gallery's interior is decorated in Arts and Crafts style, nowhere more splendidly than in the Great Hall. Above the Gothic colonnade a processional frieze painted by William Hole in 1898 serves as a 'visual encyclopedia' of famous Scots, shown in chronological order from Calgacus (the chieftain who led the Caledonian tribes into battle against the Romans) to writer and philosopher Thomas Carlyle (1795–1881). The murals on the 1st-floor balcony depict scenes from Scottish history, while the ceiling is painted with the constellations of the night sky.

Bonnie Prince Charlie

Contrast the 1750 portrait of a dashing Prince Charles Edward Stuart (1720–88), in tartan suit and Jacobite bonnet, at a time when he still had hopes of returning to Scotland to claim the throne, and the one painted towards the end of his life – exiled in Rome, an alcoholic and a broken man.

Three Oncologists

This eerie portrait by Ken Currie of three leading cancer specialists somehow captures the horror of the disease along with the sense that their achievements in treating it are a kind of alchemical mystery.

★ Top Tips

o The gallery's selection of 'trails' leaflets provide a bit of background information while leading you around the various exhibits; the Hidden Histories trail is particularly interesting.

o Free guided tours of the gallery's architecture are held at 2pm on the third Saturday of the month; book in advance by calling ☏ 0131-624 6560.

✕ Take a Break

The excellent soups and sandwiches at the gallery's **Cafe Portrait** (www.heritageportfolio.co.uk/cafes/our-cafes/cafe-portrait; 1 Queen St; mains £7-11; ◷ 10am-4.30pm; 🛜; 🚇 St Andrew Sq) make it a popular lunch spot for local office workers.

If that's too crowded, head a block west to **Dogs** (www.thedogsonline.co.uk; 110 Hanover St; mains lunch £7, dinner £12-15; ◷ noon-2.30pm & 6-10pm Mon-Fri, noon-4pm & 6-10pm Sat & Sun; ✐; 🚌 23, 27).

Top Sight
Princes Street Gardens

The beautiful Princes Street Gardens are slung between Edinburgh's Old and New Towns, and split in two by the Mound – around two million cartloads of earth that were dug out from foundations during the construction of the New Town and dumped here to provide a road link across the valley to the Old Town. The road was completed in 1830.

◎ MAP P94, B6

Princes St

admission free

🕐 dawn-dusk

🚃 Princes St

Scott Monument

The eastern half of Princes Street Gardens is dominated by the massive Gothic spire of the **Scott Monument** (www.edinburghmuseums.org.uk; East Princes Street Gardens; £5; ⏱10am-7pm Apr-Sep, to 4pm Oct-Mar; 🚌Princes St), built by public subscription in memory of novelist Sir Walter Scott after his death in 1832. The exterior is decorated with carvings of characters from his novels; inside you can see an exhibition on Scott's life, and climb the 287 steps to the top for a superb view of the city.

West End Churches

The western end of the gardens is dominated by the tower of **St John's Church** (Princes St; 🚌all Princes St buses), worth visiting for its fine Gothic Revival interior. It overlooks **St Cuthbert's Parish Church** (Lothian Rd; 🚌all Lothian Rd buses), built in the 1890s on a site of great antiquity – there has been a church here since at least the 12th century, and perhaps since the 7th century. There's a circular **watchtower** in the graveyard, a reminder of the days when graves had to be guarded against bodysnatchers (p55).

Floral Clock & Ross Bandstand

At the entrance to the western gardens on the corner of Princes St and the Mound is the Floral Clock, a working clock laid out in flowers; it was first created in 1903 and the design changes every year. In the middle of the western part of the gardens is the Ross Bandstand, a venue for open-air concerts in summer and at Hogmanay, and the stage for the famous fireworks concert during the Edinburgh International Festival (there are plans to replace the ageing bandstand with a modern concert venue).

★ Top Tips

○ The gardens are home to events throughout the year, from the Edinburgh International Festival's fireworks concert to the Christmas Market and Ferris wheel in December.

○ Spring is the time to see the flower displays at their best – in April the slopes below the castle esplanade are thick with yellow daffodils.

○ On Saturday you can buy food from the farmers market on Castle Tce, then grab a bench in the neighbouring gardens for an alfresco meal.

✕ Take a Break

The Scottish Cafe & Restaurant (p103), beneath the Royal Scottish Academy, offers the chance to enjoy traditional Scottish cuisine with a view along the eastern gardens.

Walking Tour 🥾

Charlotte Square to Calton Hill

Edinburgh's New Town is one of the world's finest Georgian cityscapes, well worthy of its Unesco World Heritage status. This walk captures the essence of the New Town's Georgian elegance, taking in its two architecturally pivotal squares, the grand townhouses of Heriot Row (complete with private gardens), and two of the city's best viewpoints, the Scott Monument and Calton Hill.

Walk Facts
Start Charlotte Sq
End Calton Hill
Length 1.5 miles; one hour

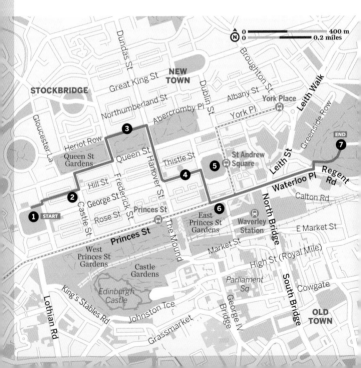

❶ Charlotte Square

Charlotte Square (p96) is a masterpiece of neoclassical design. On the north side is the museum **Georgian House** (p96), while off the southeast corner is **16 South Charlotte St**, birthplace of telephone pioneer Alexander Graham Bell.

❷ Oxford Bar

Leave the square at its northeast corner and turn right along Young St, passing the **Oxford Bar** (p107), made famous by Ian Rankin's Inspector Rebus novels. Turn left on N Castle St, right on Queen St then left again, taking a peek into the private **Queen Street Gardens**.

❸ Heriot Row

Turn right into Heriot Row, a typically elegant New Town terrace. At No 17 an inscription marks the house where writer Robert Louis Stevenson spent his childhood. It's said that the island in the pond in Queen Street Gardens (not open to the public) was the inspiration for *Treasure Island*.

❹ George Street

Go uphill to George St and turn left. This was once the centre of Edinburgh's financial industry; now the banks and offices have been taken over by designer boutiques and cocktail bars. Pop into the **Dome Grill Room** at No 14, formerly a bank, to see the ornate Georgian banking hall.

❺ St Andrew Square

The New Town's most impressive square is dominated by the **Melville Monument**, commemorating Henry Dundas (1742–1811), the most powerful Scottish politician of his time. On the far side is **Dundas House**, a Palladian mansion that houses the head office of the Royal Bank of Scotland (another magnificent domed banking hall lies within).

❻ Scott Monument

South St David St leads past **Jenners** (p93), the grand dame of Edinburgh department stores, to the **Scott Monument** (p89). Climb the 287 steps to the top for an incomparable view over **Princes Street Gardens** (p88) to the castle.

❼ Calton Hill

Head east along Princes St and Waterloo Pl to the stairs on the left, just after the side street called Calton Hill. Climb to the summit of **Calton Hill** (p97), one of Edinburgh's finest viewpoints, with a panorama that stretches from the Firth of Forth to the Pentland Hills.

Walking Tour

New Town Shopping

Shopping in the New Town offers everything from mall-crawling and traditional department stores to browsing in dinky little designer boutiques and rubbing shoulderbags with fussing fashionistas in Harvey Nicks. And all in a compact city centre that you can cover without blowing the bank on taxis or getting blisters from your Blahniks.

Walk Facts

Start Princes St
End St Andrew Sq
Length 1.5 miles; one hour

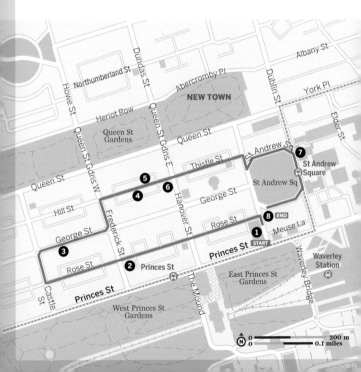

❶ Jenners

Founded in 1838, **Jenners** (www. houseoffraser.co.uk; 48 Princes St) is the grande dame of Edinburgh shopping. Its five floors stock a wide range of quality goods, both classic and contemporary (it's especially strong on designer shoes and handbags, hats, knitwear and oriental rugs) plus a food hall, hairdresser, gift-wrapping service and four cafes.

❷ Rose Street

Pedestrianised Rose St was once notorious as a pub crawl; there are still pubs, but the street is better known today for shops, mostly mainstream, which range from outdoor sports emporiums such as Cotswold Outdoor and Tiso to antique jewellery specialists like **Alistir Wood Tait** (www.alistirtait gem.co.uk; 116a Rose St).

❸ Cruise

An ornately corniced foyer leads into three floors of minimalist gallery-like decor. This **branch** (www.cruisefashion.co.uk; 94 George St) and an outlet at nearby 80 George St show off the best of mainstream designer labels including Paul Smith, Jasper Conran, Hugo Boss, Joseph Tricot, Armani and Dolce & Gabbana.

❹ 21st Century Kilts

Thistle St, Rose St's partner to the north of George St, has become an enclave of designer boutiques. **21st Century Kilts** (http://21stcenturykilts.com; 48 Thistle St) offers modern fashion kilts in a variety of fabrics, both off-the-peg and made to measure; celebrity customers include Alan Cummings, Robbie Williams and Vin Diesel.

❺ Alchemia

Made in a workshop in Fife, the jewellery on display at **Alchemia** (www.alchemia.co.uk; 37 Thistle St) is designed in Scotland and inspired by the shapes and colours of the natural world. If nothing catches your eye, you can request bespoke jewellery.

❻ Covet

Another Thistle St stalwart, **Covet** (www.thoushaltcovet.com; 20 Thistle St) has an emphasis on up-and-coming new designers from all over the world. Look for bags by Dutch label Smaak and New York designer Rebecca Minkoff, jewellery by Tatty Devine, and watches from Swedish brand Triwa.

❼ Harvey Nichols

The jewel in the crown of Edinburgh's shopping scene, **Harvey Nichols** (www.harveynichols.com; 30-34 St Andrew Sq) has four floors of designer labels and is the anchor for the Multrees Walk luxury shopping mall. Nearby you'll find boutiques by Louis Vuitton, Mulberry, Hugo Boss, Swarovski and more.

❽ Ivy on the Square

By now you'll be looking forward to a break; **The Ivy on the Square** (p102) is an ideal place for lunch, or perhaps a self-indulgent afternoon tea.

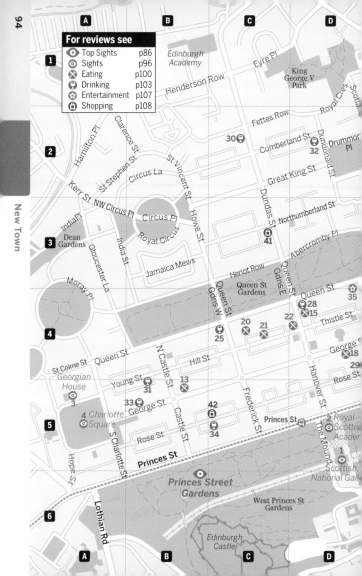

New Town

For reviews see
- ◎ Top Sights — p86
- ◎ Sights — p96
- ✖ Eating — p100
- ☕ Drinking — p103
- ✪ Entertainment — p107
- 🔒 Shopping — p108

Edinburgh Academy

Eyre Pl

King George V Park

Henderson Row

Royal Cres

Hamilton Pl

Clarence St

Fettes Row

Cumberland St

Dundonald St

Drummor Pl

30

32

St Stephen St

St Vincent St

Circus La

Great King St

Kerr St

NW Circus Pl

Howe St

Dundas St

Northumberland St

IndiaPl

Circus Pl

Royal Circus

Dean Gardens

India St

Gloucester La

Jamaica Mews

Heriot Row

41

Abercromby Pl

Moray Pl

Queen St Gdns W

Queen St Gardens

Queen St Gdns E

Queen St

35

28

15

Thistle St

20

21

22

25

George

18

St Colme St

Queen St

N Castle St

Hill St

Hanover St

29

Rose St

Georgian House

3

Young St

31

13

42

Frederick St

Princes St

2 Royal Scottis Acader

33

George St

Castle St

34

4 Charlotte Square

Rose St

S Charlotte St

Princes St

1 Scottish National Gall

Hope St

Lothian Rd

Princes Street Gardens

The Mound

Princes Street Gardens

West Princes St Gardens

Edinburgh Castle

E Claremont St

Bellevue

Bellevue Cres

Annandale St

Leith Walk

Brunswick St

1

200 m
0
0
0.1 miles

E London St

Gayfield St

43

Montgomery St

26

London St

NEW TOWN

40

39

Broughton Pl

Union St

Gayfield Sq

Elm Row

38

Windsor St

2

London Rd

12

Royal Terrace Gardens

Royal Tce

Barony St

Albany St La

23

Broughton St

Forth St

Broughton St La

16

3

Albany St

York La

Regent Gardens

York PI

Cathedral La

CC Blooms

ottish
tional
rtrait
llery

36

York Place

Elder St

St James Shopping Centre

44

Leith St

Omni Centre

Greenside Row

Calton Hill

Regent Gardens

Edinburgh Bus Station

11

Dundas House

Collective/City Observatory

6

5

National Monument

8

Calton Hill

4

t Andrew Square

10

t Andrew Square

37

24

27

7

Nelson Monument

Royal High School

19

14

Waterloo PI

9

St Andrew's House

Regent Rd

Old Calton Burial Ground

Calton Rd

Canongate Kirk

5

Edinburgh Tourist Office

17

North Bridge

New St

Waverley Bridge

Waverley Station

E Market St

Canongate (Royal Mile)

Museum of Edinburgh

Princes St Gardens

Market St

South Bridge

OLD TOWN

St Mary's St

St John St

ank St

High St (Royal Mile)

Blackfriars St

Cowgate

George IV Bridge

Holyrood Rd

6

E

F

G

H

Sights

Scottish National Gallery
GALLERY

1 ⊙ MAP P94, D5

Designed by William Playfair, this imposing classical building with its Ionic porticoes dates from 1850. Its octagonal rooms, lit by skylights, have been restored to their original Victorian decor of deep-green carpets and dark-red walls. The gallery houses an important collection of European art from the Renaissance to the post-Impressionism era, with works by Verrocchio (Leonardo da Vinci's teacher), Tintoretto, Titian, Holbein, Rubens, Van Dyck, Vermeer, El Greco, Poussin, Rembrandt, Gainsborough, Turner, Constable, Monet, Pissarro, Gauguin and Cézanne. (☎0131-624 6200; www.nationalgalleries.org; The Mound; admission free; ⊙10am-5pm Fri-Wed, to 7pm Thu; ₪all Princes St buses, ₪Princes St)

Royal Scottish Academy
GALLERY

2 ⊙ MAP P94, D5

This Greek Doric temple, with its northern pediment crowned by a seated figure of Queen Victoria, is the home of the Royal Scottish Academy. Designed by William Playfair and built between 1823 and 1836, it was originally called the Royal Institution; the RSA took over the building in 1910. The galleries display a collection of paintings, sculptures and architectural drawings by academy members dating from 1831, and they host temporary exhibitions throughout the year (fees for these vary). (☎0131-225 6671; www.royalscottishacademy.org; The Mound; admission free; ⊙10am-5pm Mon-Sat, noon-5pm Sun; ₪Princes St)

Georgian House
HISTORIC BUILDING

3 ⊙ MAP P94, A5

The National Trust for Scotland's Georgian House has been beautifully restored and furnished to show how Edinburgh's wealthy elite lived at the end of the 18th century. The walls are decorated with paintings by Allan Ramsay, Sir Henry Raeburn and Sir Joshua Reynolds, and there's a fully equipped 18th-century kitchen complete with china closet and wine cellar. (NTS; www.nts.org.uk; 7 Charlotte Sq; adult/child £8/6; ⊙10am-5pm Apr-Oct, 11am-4pm Mar & Nov, 11am-4pm Thu-Sun 1 Dec-16 Dec; ₪19, 36, 37, 41, 47)

Charlotte Square
SQUARE

4 ⊙ MAP P94, A5

At the western end of George St is Charlotte Sq, the architectural jewel of the New Town, which was designed by Robert Adam shortly before his death in 1791. The northern side of the square is Adam's masterpiece and one of the finest examples of Georgian architecture anywhere. **Bute House** (6 Charlotte Sq; ₪19, 36, 37, 41, 47), in the centre at No 6, is the official residence of Scotland's first minister. (₪19, 36, 37, 41, 47)

Calton Hill

VIEWPOINT

5 ◎ MAP P94, H4

Calton Hill (100m), which rises dramatically above the eastern end of Princes St, is Edinburgh's acropolis, its summit scattered with grandiose memorials dating mostly from the first half of the 19th century. It is also one of the best viewpoints in Edinburgh, with a panorama that takes in the castle, Holyrood, Arthur's Seat, the Firth of Forth, the New Town and the full length of Princes St. (🚌1, 4, 5, 15, 34, 45)

Collective/City Observatory

GALLERY

6 ◎ MAP P94, G4

The design of the City Observatory, built in 1818, was based on the Temple of the Winds in Athens. Its original function was to provide a precise, astronomical time-keeping service for marine navigators, but smoke from Waverley train station forced the astronomers to move to Blackford Hill in the south of Edinburgh in 1895. The observatory has been redeveloped as a stunning space for contemporary visual art, and opened to the public for the first time in its history. (📞0131-556 1264; www.collectivegallery.net; Calton Hill; admission free; 🕑10am-5pm Tue-Sun Apr-Jul & Sep, to 4pm Oct-Mar, to 6pm daily Aug; 🚌1, 4, 5, 15, 34, 45)

Edinburgh Zoo

Opened in 1913, **Edinburgh Zoo** (📞0131-334 9171; www.edinburghzoo.org.uk; 134 Corstorphine Rd; adult/child £19.50/9.95; 🕑10am-6pm Apr-Sep, to 5pm Oct & Mar, to 4pm Nov-Feb; 🚻; 🚌12, 26, 31) is one of the world's leading conservation zoos. Edinburgh's captive breeding program has helped save many endangered species, including Siberian tigers, pygmy hippos and red pandas. The main attractions are the two **giant pandas**, Tian Tian and Yang Guang, who arrived in December 2011, and the **penguin parade** (the zoo's penguins go for a walk every day at 2.15pm). The zoo is 2.5 miles west of the city centre.

Nelson Monument

MONUMENT

7 ◎ MAP P94, H4

Looking a bit like an upturned telescope – the similarity is intentional – and offering superb views over the city and across the Firth of Forth, the Nelson Monument was built to commemorate Admiral Lord Nelson's victory at Trafalgar in 1805. (www.edinburghmuseums.org.uk; Calton Hill; £5; 🕑10am-7pm Mon-Sat, noon-5pm Sun Apr-Sep, 10am-4pm Mon-Sat Oct-Mar; 🚌1, 4, 5, 15, 34, 45)

New Town
History

Between the end of the 14th century and the start of the 18th, the population of Edinburgh – still confined within the walls of the Old Town – increased from 2000 to 50,000. The tottering tenements were unsafe and occasionally collapsed, fire was an ever-present danger and the overcrowding and squalor became unbearable. There was no sewer system and household waste was disposed of by flinging it from the window into the street with a euphemistic shout of 'Gardyloo!' (from the French 'gardez l'eau' – beware of the water). Passersby replied with 'Haud yer haun'!' (Hold your hand) but were often too late. The stink that rose from the streets was ironically referred to as 'the floo'rs o' Edinburgh' (the flowers of Edinburgh).

So when the Act of Union in 1707 brought the prospect of long-term stability, the upper classes wanted healthier, more spacious living quarters, and in 1766 the Lord Provost of Edinburgh announced a competition to design an extension to the city. It was won by an unknown 23-year-old, James Craig, a self-taught architect whose elegant plan envisaged the New Town's main axis, George St, following the crest of a ridge to the north of the Old Town, with grand squares at each end. Building was restricted to just one side of Princes St and Queen St, so that the houses had views over the Firth of Forth to the north, and to the castle and Old Town to the south.

During the 18th and 19th centuries, the New Town continued to sprout squares, circuses, parks and terraces, with some of its finest neoclassical architecture designed by Robert Adam. Today it is one of the world's finest examples of a Georgian cityscape, and is part of a Unesco World Heritage Site.

National Monument MONUMENT

8 MAP P94, H4

The largest structure on the summit of Calton Hill, the National Monument was a rather over-ambitious attempt to replicate the Parthenon in Athens, and was intended to honour Scotland's dead in the Napoleonic Wars. Construction – paid for by public subscription – began in 1822, but funds ran dry after only 12 columns had been erected. It became known locally as 'Edinburgh's Disgrace'. (Calton Hill; 1, 4, 5, 15, 34, 45)

Old Calton Burial Ground CEMETERY

9 MAP P94, G4

One of Edinburgh's many atmospheric old cemeteries, Old Calton is dominated by the tall black obelisk of the **Political Martyrs' Monument**, which commemorates those who suffered in the fight for electoral reform in the 1790s. In the southern corner is the massive cylindrical grey stone **tomb of David Hume** (1711–76), Scotland's most famous philosopher.

Hume was a noted atheist, prompting rumours that he had made a Faustian pact with the devil; after his death his friends held a vigil at the tomb for eight nights, burning candles and firing pistols into the darkness lest evil spirits come to bear away his soul. (Waterloo Pl; 🚌1, 4, 5, 15, 34, 45)

St Andrew Square
SQUARE

10 ◎ MAP P94, E4

Though not as architecturally distinguished as its sister Charlotte Square (p96), at the opposite end of George St, St Andrew Sq is dominated by the fluted column of the **Melville Monument**, commemorating Henry Dundas, 1st Viscount Melville (1742–1811). Popular restaurants line the south side, while the east side is dominated by 2018's **Edinburgh Grand** luxury-apartments development. On summer afternoons the garden in the middle fills with lunching office workers who sip coffee from the square's espresso bar. (🚊St Andrew Sq)

Dundas House
HISTORIC BUILDING

11 ◎ MAP P94, E4

The impressive Palladian mansion of Dundas House, built between 1772 and 1774 on the eastern side of St Andrew Sq, was built for Sir Laurence Dundas (1712–81). It has been the head office of the Royal

St Andrew Square and Melville Monument

Bank of Scotland since 1825 and has a spectacular domed banking hall dating from 1857 (you can nip inside for a look). (St Andrew Sq; 🚇St Andrew Sq)

Eating

Gardener's Cottage
SCOTTISH ££

12 🍴 MAP P94, H2

This country cottage in the heart of the city, bedecked with flowers and fairy lights, offers one of Edinburgh's most interesting dining experiences – two tiny rooms with communal tables made of salvaged timber, and a set menu based on fresh local produce (most of the vegetables and fruit are from its own organic garden). Bookings essential; brunch served at weekends. (📞0131-558 1221; www.thegardenerscottage.co; 1 Royal Terrace Gardens, London Rd; 4-course lunch £21, 7-course dinner £50; 🕐noon-2pm & 5-10pm Mon-Fri, 10am-2pm & 5-10pm Sat & Sun; 🚌all London Rd buses)

Contini
ITALIAN ££

13 🍴 MAP P94, B5

A palatial Georgian banking hall enlivened by fuchsia-pink banners and lampshades is home to this lively, family-friendly Italian bar and restaurant, where the emphasis is on fresh, authentic ingredients (produce imported weekly from Milan; homemade bread and pasta) and the uncomplicated enjoyment of food. (📞0131-225

1550; www.contini.com/contini-george-street; 103 George St; mains £14-18; 🕐8am-10pm Mon-Fri, 10am-10.30pm Sat, 11am-8pm Sun; 🛜🍴♿; 🚌all Princes St buses)

Dishoom
INDIAN ££

14 🍴 MAP P94, E4

Dishoom is a new addition to Edinburgh's dining scene and the mini-chain's first opening outside London. Inspired by the Irani cafes of Bombay, this is exquisite Indian street food served in upmarket surroundings; the breakfasts, including the signature bacon naan, are legendary. Hugely popular – book well ahead, or be prepared to queue for a table. (📞0131-202 6406; www.dishoom.com/edinburgh; 3a St Andrew Sq; 🕐8am-11pm Mon-Wed, to midnight Thu & Fri, 9am-midnight Sat, 9am-11pm Sun; 🛜; 🚇St Andrew Sq)

Urban Angel
CAFE £

15 🍴 MAP P94, D4

A wholesome deli that puts the emphasis on Fairtrade, organic and locally sourced produce, Urban Angel is also a delightfully informal cafe-bistro that serves all-day brunch (porridge with honey, French toast, eggs Benedict), mix-and-match salads, and a wide range of light, snacky meals. (📞0131-225 6215; www.urban-angel.co.uk; 121 Hanover St; mains £7-11; 🕐8am-5pm Mon-Fri, 9am-5pm Sat & Sun; 🍴♿; 🚌23, 27)

Paul Kitching 21212 FRENCH £££

16 ⊗ MAP P94, H3

A grand Georgian townhouse on the side of Calton Hill is the elegant setting for one of Edinburgh's Michelin-starred restaurants. Divine decor by Timorous Beasties and Ralph Lauren provides the backdrop to an exquisitely prepared five-course dinner (£85) that changes weekly and features fresh, seasonal delights. (☎0131-523 1030; www.21212restaurant.co.uk; 3 Royal Tce; 3-course lunch/dinner from £32/70; ⏱noon-1.45pm & 7-9pm Tue-Sat; 🛜; 🚌all London Rd buses)

Number One SCOTTISH £££

17 ⊗ MAP P94, F5

This is the stylish and sophisticated chatelaine of Edinburgh's city-centre restaurants, all gold-and-velvet elegance with a Michelin star sparkling on her tiara. The food is top-notch modern Scottish and the service is just on the right side of fawning. (☎0131-557 6727; www.roccofortehotels.com/hotels-and-resorts/the-balmoral-hotel/restaurants-and-bars/number-one; Balmoral Hotel, 1 Princes St; 3-course dinner £80; ⏱6.30-10pm Mon-Thu, 6-10pm Fri-Sun; 🛜; 🚌all Princes St buses)

Dome SCOTTISH ££

18 ⊗ MAP P94, D4

Housed in the magnificent neoclassical former headquarters of the Commercial Bank, with a lofty glass-domed ceiling, pillared arches and mosaic-tiled floor, the Grill Room at the Dome is one of

Exterior of Dome restaurant

The One O'Clock Gun

On Princes St you can tell locals and visitors apart by their reaction to the sudden explosion that rips through the air each day at one o'clock. Locals check their watches, while visitors shy like startled ponies. It's the One O'Clock Gun, fired from Mills Mount Battery on the castle battlements at 1pm sharp every day except Sunday.

The gun's origins date from the mid-19th century, when the accurate setting of a ship's chronometer was essential for safe navigation. The city authorities installed a time-signal on top of the Nelson Monument that was visible to ships anchored in the Firth of Forth. The gun was added as an audible signal that could be used when rain or mist obscured the visual signal. An interesting little exhibition in the Museum of Edinburgh (p52) details the gun's history and workings.

the city's most impressive dining rooms. The menu is solidly modern Scottish, with great steaks, seafood and venison. Reservations strongly recommended. (☎0131-624 8624; www.thedomeedinburgh.com; 14 George St; mains £15-28; ⏱10am-late; 🚇St Andrew Sq)

Ivy on the Square

BRITISH ££

20 MAP P94, E4

The first Scottish outpost of London's famous celebrity haunt, the Ivy in Covent Garden, this classy but informal brasserie serves up traditional British dishes, from eggs Benedict for brunch through afternoon tea to the Ivy's classic dinner of shepherd's pie or steak, egg and chips. (☎0131-526 4777; https://theivyedinburgh.com; 6 St Andrew Sq; mains £13-19; ⏱8am-midnight Mon-Sat, 9am-10.30pm Sun; 🛜; 🚇St Andrew Sq)

Cafe St Honore

FRENCH £££

20 MAP P94, C4

This intimate French restaurant is the ideal place for a romantic dinner. Service is discreet, the menu is sumptuous and the wine list is long. You can get a two-course dinner for £14.50, and a three-course set dinner for £25.50. (☎0131-226 2211; www.cafesthonore.com; 34 Thistle St Lane NW; mains £16-25; ⏱noon-2pm & 6-10pm; 🚇Princes St)

Bon Vivant

BISTRO ££

21 MAP P94, C4

Candlelight reflected in the warm glow of polished wood makes for an intimate atmosphere in this New Town favourite. The food is superb value for this part of town, offering a range of tapas-style 'bites' as well as standard main courses, with a changing menu of seasonal, locally sourced dishes such as cod fillet with bacon and mussel cream. (📞 0131-225 3275; http://bonvantedinburgh.co.uk; 55 Thistle St; mains £13-17; 🕐 noon-10pm; 🛜; 🚌 23, 27)

Scottish Cafe & Restaurant
SCOTTISH ££

This appealing modern restaurant – part of the Scottish National Gallery complex (see 2 🔵 Map p94, D5) – has picture windows providing a view along Princes Street Gardens (p88). Try traditional Scottish dishes such as Cullen skink (smoked-haddock soup) and leek-and-potato soup, or seasonal, sustainably sourced produce including smoked salmon and trout, free-range chicken and pork. (📞 0131-225 1550; www.contini.com/scottish-cafe-and-restaurant; The Mound; mains £10-15; 🕐 9am-5pm Mon-Sat, to 7pm Thu, 10am-5pm Sun; 🛜🚻; 🚌 Princes St)

Henderson's
VEGETARIAN £

22 🔴 MAP P94, D4

Established in 1962, Henderson's is the grandmother of Edinburgh's vegetarian restaurants. The food is mostly organic and guaranteed GM-free, and special dietary requirements can be catered for. Trays and counter service lend something of a 1970s canteen feel to the place (in a good, nostalgic way), and the daily salads and hot dishes are as popular as ever.

Right around the corner on Thistle St is Henderson's Vegan bistro. (📞 0131-225 2131; www.hendersons

ofedinburgh.co.uk; 94 Hanover St; mains £7-14; 🕐 8.30am-8.45pm Mon-Thu, to 9.15pm Fri & Sat, 10.30am-4pm Sun; 🛜🚻🚻; 🚌 23, 27)

Seasons
SCANDINAVIAN ££

23 🔴 MAP P94, F2

The Swedish chef at Seasons creates a dynamic fusion of Scottish and Scandinavian influences, trading in the traditional à la carte menu for a set list of seasonal produce from which your meal will be created (you can point out anything you don't fancy), then beautifully garnished with foraged ingredients and edible flowers. (📞 0131-466 9851; www.seasons tasting.com; 36 Broughton St; 5-course tasting menu £40; 🕐 5-9.30pm Wed & Thu, noon-2.30pm & 5-9.30pm Fri-Sun; 🛜; 🚌 8)

Drinking

Café Royal Circle Bar
PUB

24 🔴 MAP P94, F4

Perhaps *the* classic Edinburgh pub, the Café Royal's main claims to fame are its magnificent oval bar and its Doulton tile portraits of famous Victorian inventors. Sit at the bar or claim one of the cosy leather booths beneath the stained-glass windows, and choose from the seven real ales on tap. (📞 0131-556 1884; www.cafe royaledinburgh.co.uk; 17 W Register St; 🕐 11am-11pm Mon-Wed, to midnight Thu, to 1am Fri & Sat, to 10pm Sun; 🛜; 🚌 Princes St)

New Town Drinking

Bohemian Broughton

The lively, bohemian district of Broughton, centred on Broughton St at the northeastern corner of the New Town, is the focus of Edinburgh's gay scene and home to many good bars, cafes and restaurants. **CC Blooms** (Map p94, G3; ☎0131-556 9331; http://ccblooms.co.uk; 23 Greenside Pl; ⏰11am-3am; 🛜; 🚌all Leith Walk buses), opposite the top end of Broughton St, is the city's biggest gay club.

Lucky Liquor Co   COCKTAIL BAR

25 🚇 MAP P94, C4

This tiny, black-and-white bar is all about the number 13: 13 bottles of base spirit are used to create a daily menu of 13 cocktails. The result is a playful list with some unusual flavours, such as tonka-bean liqueur, pea purée and lavender absinthe (though not all in the same glass!), served by a fun and friendly crew. (☎0131-226 3976; www.luckyliquorco.com; 39a Queen St; ⏰4pm-1am; 🚌24, 29, 42)

Joseph Pearce's   PUB

26 🚇 MAP P94, H2

This traditional Victorian pub has been remodelled and given a new lease of life by the Swedish owners. It's a real hub of the local community, with good food (very family friendly before 5pm), a relaxed atmosphere, and events like Monday-night Scrabble games and August crayfish parties. (☎0131-556 4140; www.bodabar.com/joseph-pearces; 23 Elm Row; ⏰11am-midnight Sun-Thu, to 1am Fri & Sat; 🛜🚻; 🚌all Leith Walk buses)

Guildford Arms   PUB

27 🚇 MAP P94, F4

Located in a side alley off the east end of Princes St, the Guildford is a classic Victorian pub full of polished mahogany, brass and ornate cornices. The range of real ales is excellent – try to get a table in the unusual upstairs gallery, with a view over the sea of drinkers below. (☎0131-556 4312; www.guildfordarms.com; 1 W Register St; ⏰11am-11pm Mon-Thu, to 11.30pm Fri & Sat, 12.30-11pm Sun; 🛜; 🚌St Andrew Sq)

Bramble   COCKTAIL BAR

28 🚇 MAP P94, D4

One of those places that easily earn the sobriquet 'best-kept secret', Bramble is an unmarked cellar bar (just an inconspicuous brass nameplate beneath a dry-cleaner's shop) where a maze of stone and brick hideaways conceals what is arguably the city's best cocktail venue. No beer taps, no fuss, just expertly mixed drinks. (☎0131-226 6343; www.bramblebar.co.uk; 16a Queen St; ⏰4pm-1am; 🚌23, 27)

Abbotsford

PUB

29 🚌 MAP P94, D4

One of the few pubs in Rose St that has retained its Edwardian splendour, the Abbotsford has long been a hang-out for writers, actors, journalists and media people, and has many loyal regulars. Dating from 1902, and named after Sir Walter Scott's country house, the pub's centrepiece is a splendid mahogany island bar. Good selection of real ales. (📞0131-225 5276; www.theabbotsford.com; 3 Rose St; ⏰11am-11pm Mon-Thu, to midnight Fri & Sat, 12.30-11pm Sun; 🛜; 🚌all Princes St buses)

Clark's Bar

PUB

30 🚌 MAP P94, C2

A century old and still going strong, Clark's caters to a clientele of real-ale aficionados, football fans (there are three TVs), local office workers and loyal regulars, who appreciate an old-fashioned, no-frills pub with lots of wood panelling and polished brass, and cosy little back rooms for convivial storytelling. (📞0131-556 1067; www. facebook.com/ClarksBarEdinburgh; 142 Dundas St; ⏰noon-11.30pm Sun-Thu, to 12.30am Fri & Sat; 🛜🐾; 🚌23, 27)

Tigerlily (p107)

Literary Edinburgh

Sir Walter Scott

The writer most deeply associated with Edinburgh is undoubtedly Sir Walter Scott (1771–1832), Scotland's greatest and most prolific novelist, best remembered for classic tales such as *The Antiquary, The Heart of Midlothian, Ivanhoe, Redgauntlet* and *Castle Dangerous*. He lived at various New Town addresses before moving to his country house at Abbotsford.

Robert Louis Stevenson

Robert Louis Stevenson (1850–94) was born at 8 Howard Pl, in the New Town, into a family of famous lighthouse engineers. Stevenson is known and loved around the world for stories such as *Kidnapped, Catriona, Treasure Island, The Master of Ballantrae* and *The Strange Case of Dr Jekyll and Mr Hyde*, many of which have been made into successful films. The most popular and enduring is *Treasure Island* (1883), which has been translated into many different languages and has never been out of print.

Muriel Spark

No list of Edinburgh novelists would be complete without mention of Dame Muriel Spark (1918–2006), who was born in Edinburgh and educated at James Gillespie's High School for Girls, an experience that provided material for her best-known novel *The Prime of Miss Jean Brodie* (1961), a shrewd portrait of 1930s Edinburgh. Dame Muriel was a prolific writer; her 22nd novel, *The Finishing School*, was published in 2004 when she was 86.

Contemporary Writers

Walk into any bookshop in Edinburgh and you'll find a healthy 'Scottish Fiction' section, with recently published works by best-selling Edinburgh authors such as Candia McWilliam, Ian Rankin, Sara Sheridan, Alexander McCall Smith and Irvine Welsh.

Ian Rankin's Rebus novels are dark, engrossing mysteries that explore the darker side of Scotland's capital city, filled with sharp dialogue, telling detail and three-dimensional characters.

Although she was born in England, the publishing phenomenon that is JK Rowling famously began her career by penning the first Harry Potter adventure while nursing a coffee in various Edinburgh cafes; she still lives in Scotland.

Oxford Bar PUB

31 MAP P94, B5

The Oxford is that rarest of things: a real pub for real people, with no 'theme', no music, no frills and no pretensions. 'The Ox' has been immortalised by Ian Rankin, author of the Inspector Rebus novels, whose fictional detective is a regular here. Occasional live folk music. (0131-539 7119; www.oxfordbar.co.uk; 8 Young St; noon-midnight Mon-Thu, 11am-1am Fri & Sat, 12.30-11pm Sun; all Princes St buses)

Cumberland Bar PUB

32 MAP P94, D2

Immortalised as the stereotypical New Town pub in Alexander Mc-Call Smith's serialised novel *44 Scotland Street,* the Cumberland has an authentic, traditional wood-brass-and-mirrors look (despite being relatively new) and serves well-looked-after, cask-conditioned ales and a wide range of malt whiskies. There's also a pleasant little beer garden. (0131-558 3134; www.cumberlandbar.co.uk; 1-3 Cumberland St; noon-midnight Mon-Wed, to 1am Thu-Sat, 11am-11pm Sun; 23, 27)

Tigerlily COCKTAIL BAR

33 MAP P94, B5

Swirling textured wallpapers, glittering chain-mail curtains, crystal chandeliers, and plush pink and gold sofas have won a cluster of design awards for this boutique-hotel bar, where sharp suits and stiletto heels line the banquettes. There's a huge list of expertly mixed cocktails, plus a range of Scottish craft beers on tap. (0131-225 5005; www.tigerlily edinburgh.co.uk/edinburgh-bar; 125 George St; 11am-1am; all Princes St buses)

Kenilworth PUB

34 MAP P94, C5

A gorgeous Edwardian drinking palace complete with original fittings – tile floors, mahogany circle bar and gantry, ornate mirrors and gas lamps – the Kenilworth was Edinburgh's original gay bar in the 1970s. Today it attracts a mixed crowd of all ages, and serves a good range of real ales and malt whiskies. (0131-226 1773; www.nicholsonspubs.co.uk; 152-154 Rose St; noon-11pm Mon-Thu, noon-midnight Fri, 11am-midnight Sat, 11am-11pm Sun; Princes St)

Entertainment

Jam House LIVE MUSIC

35 MAP P94, D3

The brainchild of rhythm-and-blues pianist and TV personality Jools Holland, the Jam House is set in a former BBC TV studio and offers a combination of fine dining and live jazz and blues performances. Admission is for over-21s only, and there's a smart-casual dress code. (0131-220 2321; www.thejamhouse.com; 5 Queen St; from £4; 6pm-3am Fri & Sat; St Andrew Sq)

Stand Comedy Club COMEDY

36 ⭐ MAP P94, E3

The Stand, founded in 1995, is Edinburgh's main independent comedy venue. It's an intimate cabaret bar with performances every night and a free Sunday lunchtime show. (☎ 0131-558 7272; www.thestand.co.uk; 5 York Pl; tickets £3-18; ⏱from 7.30pm Mon-Sat, from 12.30pm Sun; 🚇St Andrew Sq)

Voodoo Rooms LIVE MUSIC

37 ⭐ MAP P94, E4

Decadent decor of black leather, ornate plasterwork and gilt detailing creates a stylish setting for this complex of bars and performance spaces above the Café Royal (p103) that hosts everything from classic soul and Motown to blues nights, jam sessions and live local bands. (☎ 0131-556 7060; www.thevoodoorooms.com; 19a W Register St; free-£20; ⏱4pm-1am Mon-Thu, noon-1am Fri-Sun; 🚇St Andrew Sq)

Shopping

Valvona & Crolla FOOD & DRINKS

38 🔒 MAP P94, G2

The acknowledged queen of Edinburgh delicatessens, established during the 1930s, Valvona & Crolla is packed with Mediterranean goodies, including a superb choice of fine wines. It also has a good cafe. (☎ 0131-556 6066; www.valvonacrolla.co.uk; 19 Elm Row; ⏱8.30am-6pm Mon-Thu, 8am-8pm Fri & Sat, 10am-5pm Sun; 🚇all Leith Walk buses)

Late Shopping Days

Most shops in Edinburgh open late on Thursday, till 7pm or 8pm. Many city-centre stores extend their late opening to all weekdays during the Edinburgh Festival in August, and during the three weeks before Christmas.

Curiouser and Curiouser DESIGN

39 🔒 MAP P94, F2

A quirky independent boutique on hip Broughton St, selling everything from art prints to jewellery, homewares, stationery and books. The focus is on excellent design, with pieces by local and international artists, and prices that won't break the bank. Perfect for gifts and browsing. (☎ 0131-556 1866; www.curiouserandcuriouser.com; 93 Broughton St; ⏱10am-6pm Mon-Sat, noon-5pm Sun; 🚇8)

Life Story HOMEWARES

40 🔒 MAP P94, E2

If you like your design stores grown up, Scandi inspired, and accompanied by coffee and cake served in elegant crockery, head to this shop, where you'll find quality homewares, accessories and jewellery. (☎ 0131-629 9699; www.lifestoryshop.com; 53 London St; ⏱10.30am-5.30pm Wed-Fri, to 6pm Sat, 11am-5pm Sun; 🚇8)

Scottish Gallery

ARTS & CRAFTS

41 🔒 MAP P94, C3

Home to Edinburgh's leading art dealers Aitken Dott, this private gallery exhibits and sells paintings by contemporary Scottish artists and the masters of the late 19th and early 20th centuries (including the Scottish Colourists), as well as a wide range of ceramics, glassware, jewellery and textiles. (☎0131-558 1200; www.scottish-gallery.co.uk; 16 Dundas St; ⏱10am-6pm Mon-Fri, to 4pm Sat; 🚌23, 27)

Palenque

JEWELLERY

42 🔒 MAP P94, C5

Palenque is a treasure trove of contemporary silver jewellery and handcrafted accessories made using ceramics, textiles and metalwork. (☎0131-225 7194; www.palenquejewellery.co.uk; 99 Rose St; ⏱9.30am-5.30pm Mon-Sat, 11am-5pm Sun; 🚋Princes St)

McNaughtan's Bookshop

BOOKS

43 🔒 MAP P94, G2

The maze of shelves at McNaughtan's basement bookshop – established in 1957 – houses a broad spectrum of general secondhand and antiquarian books, with good selections of Scottish, history, travel, art and architecture, and children's books. (☎0131-556 5897; www.mcnaughtansbookshop.com; 3a-4a Haddington Pl; ⏱11am-5pm Tue-Sat; 🚌all Leith Walk buses)

John Lewis

DEPARTMENT STORE

44 🔒 MAP P94, F3

Remaining open while the new Edinburgh St James development (opening 2020) takes shape around it, this is the place to go for good-value clothing and household goods. (☎0131-556 9121; www.johnlewis.com; St James Centre, Leith St; ⏱9am-6pm Mon-Wed & Fri, to 8pm Thu, to 6.30pm Sat, 10am-6pm Sun; 🚋York Pl)

Explore ◈

West End & Dean Village

Edinburgh's West End is an extension of the New Town, with elegant Georgian terraces, garden squares and an enclave of upmarket shops along William and Stafford Sts. It takes in the Exchange district, now the city's financial powerhouse, and Lothian Rd's theatre quarter, and in the west tumbles into the valley of the Water of Leith to meet picturesque Dean Village.

Devote an hour to browsing the independent boutiques of Stafford and William Sts before heading down to pretty Dean Village (p115). Follow the Water of Leith Walkway upstream to the Scottish National Gallery of Modern Art (p112), and plan on having lunch at Cafe Modern One (p113).

Spend a couple of hours admiring the modern masterpieces at the gallery's two major exhibition spaces, allowing time to explore the sculptures and landscape art in the grounds. Then head back uphill to the West End via Belford Rd and Palmerston Pl for a cocktail at the Voyage of Buck (p118), followed by fine Scottish cuisine at Castle Terrace (p115).

Getting There & Around

🚌 Lothian buses 3, 4, 12, 25, 26, 31, 33 and 44 head west from Princes St to the West End, going along Shandwick Pl to Haymarket. For Dean Village, take bus 13 from Hanover St, or buses 19, 36, 37, 41 or 47 from George St to Dean Bridge and walk down Bell's Brae.

🚌 Links the airport with the city centre, passing through the neighbourhood with stops at Haymarket and West End.

Neighbourhood Map on p114

View of Dean Village RICHIE CHAN/SHUTTERSTOCK ©

Top Sight 📷

Scottish National Gallery of Modern Art

Edinburgh's gallery of modern art is split between two impressive neoclassical buildings surrounded by landscaped grounds. As well as showcasing a stunning collection of paintings by the popular, post-Impressionist Scottish Colourists, the gallery is the starting point for a walk along the Water of Leith.

◎ MAP P114, A2

📞 0131-624 6200

www.nationalgalleries.org

75 Belford Rd

admission free

🕐 10am-5pm

🚌 13

Modern One

The main collection, known as Modern One, concentrates on 20th-century art, with various European movements represented by the likes of Matisse, Picasso, Kirchner, Magritte, Miró, Mondrian and Giacometti. American and English artists are also represented, but most space is given to Scottish painters – from the Scottish Colourists of the early 20th century to contemporary artists.

Modern Two

Directly across Belford Rd from Modern One, another neoclassical mansion (formerly an orphanage) houses the gallery's annexe, Modern Two, which is home to a large collection of sculpture and graphic art created by Edinburgh-born artist Sir Eduardo Paolozzi. One of the 1st-floor rooms houses a recreation of Paolozzi's studio, while the rest of the building stages temporary exhibitions of modern art.

The Grounds

The gallery's collection extends to the surrounding grounds, featuring sculptures by Henry Moore, Rachel Whiteread, Julian Opie and Barbara Hepworth, among others. There's also a sensuous 'landform artwork' by Charles Jencks, and the **Pig Rock Bothy**, a rustic timber performance and exhibition space created in 2014 as part of the **Bothy Project** (www.thebothyproject.org).

Water of Leith

A footpath and stairs at the rear of the gallery lead down to the Water of Leith Walkway. This was the setting for **6 Times**, a sculptural project by Antony Gormley consisting of six human figures standing at various points along the river. All except the first (sprouting from the pavement at the gallery entrance) and the last (standing on a jetty in Leith) have been placed in storage until a way can be found to prevent them from falling over when the river floods.

★ Top Tips

o A free shuttle bus runs between the Scottish National Gallery and the National Portrait Gallery, with hourly departures from 11am to 4pm.

o On Saturday the gallery runs special tours and workshops designed for children; check the website (under Events) for details.

✗ Take a Break

Cafe Modern One (www.heritageportfolio.co.uk/cafes; 75 Belford Rd; mains £5-7; ⏰ 9am-4.30pm Mon-Fri, 10am-4.30pm Sat & Sun; 🛜 🚻 ; 🚌 13) has a terrace overlooking the sculptures in the grounds; **Cafe Modern Two** (www.heritageportfolio.co.uk/cafes; 72 Belford Rd; mains £6-9; ⏰ 10am-4.30pm; 🛜 🚻 ; 🚌 13) is based on a belle époque Viennese coffee house. Both serve cakes and coffee, plus hot lunch dishes from noon till 2.30pm.

West End & Dean Village

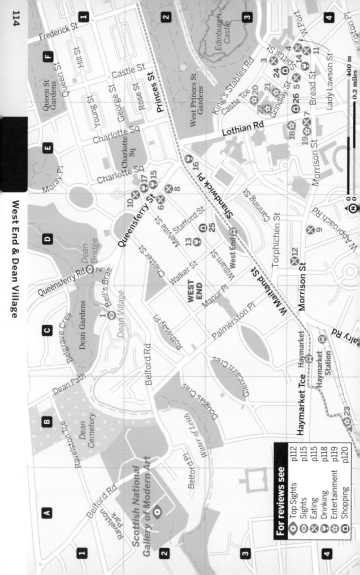

Frederick St

Hill St

Queen St Gardens

Queen St

Castle St

Young St

George St

Rose St

Princes St

Charlotte Sq

Charlotte Sq

Moray Pl

Queensferry St

Stafford St

Melville St

Queensferry Rd

Dean Bridge

Bell's Brae

Dean Village

Dean Gardens

Belgrave Cres

Ravelston Tce

Dean Cemetery

Belford Rd

Dean Path

Douglas Cres

Water of Leith

Belford Pl

Belford Rd

Ravelston Park

Scottish National Gallery of Modern Art

Chester St

Walker St

Rothesay Pl

Manor Pl

Palmerston Pl

Glencairn Cres

WEST END

William St

West End

Maitland St

Torphichen St

Canning St

Morrison St

Haymarket Tce

Haymarket

Haymarket Station

Dalry Rd

W Approach Rd

Shandwick Pl

Lothian Rd

West Princes St Gardens

West Princes St Gardens

Edinburgh Castle

King's Stables Rd

Castle Tce

Spittal St

W Port

Grindlay St

Bread St

Lady Lawson St

Morrison St

Castle St

Frederick St

Queen St

Edinburgh Castle

Thistle Pl

400 m
0.2 miles

For reviews see	
◆ Top Sights	p112
◎ Sights	p115
✕ Eating	p115
◷ Drinking	p118
☆ Entertainment	p119
⊕ Shopping	p120

Sights

Dean Village AREA

1 ◎ MAP P114, C1

Set in the valley that runs beneath the Dean Bridge ('dene' is a Scots word for valley), Dean Village was founded as a milling community by the canons of Holyrood Abbey in the 12th century, and by 1700 there were 11 water mills here, grinding grain for flour. One of the old mill buildings has been converted into flats, and the village is now an attractive residential area, with walkways along the river. (🚌19, 36, 37, 41, 47)

Dean Bridge BRIDGE

2 ◎ MAP P114, D1

Designed by Thomas Telford and built between 1829 and 1832 to allow the New Town to expand to the northwest, the Dean Bridge vaults gracefully over the narrow, steep-sided valley of the Water of Leith. It soon became notorious as a suicide spot – it soars 27m above the river – and in 1912 the parapets were raised to deter jumpers. (🚌19, 36, 37, 41, 47)

Eating

Castle Terrace SCOTTISH £££

3 🍴 MAP P114, F3

It was little more than a year after opening in 2010 that Castle Terrace was awarded a Michelin star under chef-patron Dominic Jack (the star was lost in 2015).

The menu is seasonal and applies honed Parisian skills to the finest of local produce, be it Ayrshire pork, Aberdeenshire lamb or Newhaven crab – even the cheese in the sauces is Scottish. (📞0131-229 1222; www.castleterracerestaurant.com; 33-35 Castle Tce; 3-course lunch/dinner £33/70; ⏱noon-2.15pm & 6.30-10pm Tue-Sat; 🚌2)

Timberyard SCOTTISH £££

4 🍴 MAP P114, F4

Ancient, worn floorboards, cast-iron pillars, exposed joists, and tables made from slabs of old mahogany create a rustic, retro atmosphere in this slow-food restaurant where the accent is on locally sourced produce from artisan growers and foragers. Typical dishes include seared scallop with leek, fennel and cured egg yolk, and roast quail with salsify and thyme. (📞0131-221 1222; www.timberyard.co; 10 Lady Lawson St; 4-course lunch or dinner £55; ⏱noon-2pm & 5.30-9.30pm Tue-Sat; 🛜👶; 🚌2, 300)

Kanpai Sushi JAPANESE ££

5 🍴 MAP P114, F4

What is arguably Edinburgh's best sushi restaurant impresses with its minimalist interior, fresh, top-quality fish and elegantly presented dishes – the squid tempura comes in a delicate woven basket, while the sashimi combo is presented as a flower arrangement in an ice-filled stoneware bowl. Bookings recommended.

Edinburgh Farmers Market

This **market** (☎0131-652 5940; www.edinburghfarmersmarket. com; Castle Tce; ⏱9am-2pm Sat; ☒all Lothian Rd buses) is a colourful weekly event that attracts stallholders who sell everything from wild boar, venison and home-cured pedigree bacon to organic bread, free-range eggs, honey and handmade soap.

(☎0131-228 1602; www.kanpaisushi. co.uk; 8-10 Grindlay St; mains £9-15, sushi per piece £4-10; ⏱noon-2.30pm & 5-10.30pm Tue-Sat; ☒all Lothian Rd buses)

L'Escargot Blanc   FRENCH ££

6 ⊗ MAP P114, D2

This superb neighbourhood bistro, with French chef and wait staff, and two thirds of its top-quality produce sourced in Scotland (one third imported from France), is a true 'Auld Alliance' of culinary cultures. Choose from classics such as escargots in garlic butter, *coq au vin* (made with free-range Scottish chicken), and perfectly prepared Scottish rib-eye steak with cognac sauce. (☎0131-226 1890; www.lescargotblanc.co.uk; 17 Queensferry St; mains £15-25; ⏱noon-2.30pm & 5.30-10pm Mon-Thu, noon-3pm & 5.30-10.30pm Fri & Sat; 👪; ☒19, 36, 37, 41, 47)

Shebeen   SOUTH AFRICAN ££

7 ⊗ MAP P114, E4

This snugly rustic restaurant takes pride in an extremely meaty menu, which begins with Fanagalo – a sharing platter of ribs, *boerowors* (South African sausage), *frikedelle* (meatballs), pork belly and chicken wings served in a wooden pail (literally a bucket of meat!) – and moves on to a burger topped with beef brisket, and some of the finest steaks in the city. (☎0131-629 0261; www.shebeenbar.co.uk; 8 Morrison St; mains £12-27; ⏱5-10pm Sun-Thu, noon-10pm Fri & Sat; ☒all Tollcross buses)

Maison Bleue at Home   FUSION ££

8 ⊗ MAP P114, E2

Light, bright and modern, Home mixes social purpose with quality food. The globe-spanning menu includes steaks, tagines, gumbo and posh mac 'n' cheese. Diners can pay meals forward (to be claimed by homeless people), and 100% of profits go to charity. (☎0131-220 0773; www.home-restaurant.co.uk; 7-8 Queensferry St; mains £15-32; ⏱noon-3pm & 5-10pm; ☒19, 36, 37, 47)

McKirdy's Steakhouse   SCOTTISH £££

9 ⊗ MAP P114, D4

The McKirdy brothers – owners of a local butcher business established in 1895 – have cut out the middleman and now run one of Edinburgh's best steakhouses.

The friendly staff here serves up starters – such as haggis with Drambuie sauce – and juicy, perfectly cooked steaks, from rump to T-bone. There's a two-course early dinner (until 6.30pm) for £15. (☏0131-229 6660; www.mckirdys steakhouse.co.uk; 151 Morrison St; mains £13-30; ⏰5.30-10pm Sun-Thu, 5-10.30pm Fri & Sat; 🛜🚼; 🚌2)

La P'tite Folie

FRENCH ££

 10 ⊗ MAP P114, D2

Housed in an unusual, Tudor-lookalike building, the upstairs dining room in this French-style bistro has a pleasantly clubbish feel, with candlelight, polished wood and leaded windows – try to grab the table in the little corner turret with its view of the spires of St Mary's Cathedral. (☏0131-225 8678; www. laptitefolie.co.uk; 9 Randolph Pl; mains £16-22; ⏰noon-3pm & 6-10pm Mon-Thu, to 11pm Fri & Sat; 🛜🚼; 🚌19, 36, 37, 41, 47)

Lovecrumbs

CAFE £

11 ⊗ MAP P114, F4

Serving up Edinburgh's most creative and beautiful bakes, Lovecrumbs is a shabby-chic cafe popular with students and hipsters. Cakes and tarts are presented in a vintage dresser, and the artisan Steampunk coffee and the hot chocolate by Coco Chocolatier are second to none. Anyone for lemon-and-lavender cake with a rose-and-cardamom hot chocolate? (☏0131-629 0626; www. lovecrumbs.co.uk; 155 West Port; mains £3-6; ⏰9am-6pm Mon-Fri, 9.30am-6pm Sat, noon-6pm Sun; 🚌2)

West End & Dean Village Eating

Dean Bridge (p115)

Cafe Milk
CAFE £

12 🍴 MAP P114, D4

This is fast food with a conscience – natural, nutritious, locally sourced and freshly prepared, from organic porridge to courgette, lemon and feta fritters, and North Indian dhal with rice or flatbread. Take away, or sit in and soak up the retro vibe amid old Formica tables, battered school benches, enamel plates and junk-shop cutlery stacked in golden-syrup tins. (📞0131-629 6022; www.cafemilk.co.uk; 232 Morrison St; mains £6-9; ⏱7.30am-4pm Mon-Fri, 8am-4pm Sat, 8am-3pm Sun; 🛜🍴; 🚇Haymarket)

Drinking

Voyage of Buck
BAR

13 🍺 MAP P114, D2

You'll need to take a seat to peruse the 25-page drinks menu at this 'concept pub', themed around the exploits of a fictitious Victorian adventurer called Buck Clarence. Both the decor and the cocktails are inspired by the cities Buck visited on his supposed travels, including Paris, Cairo, Casablanca and Delhi – it's all tongue-in-cheek, a bit decadent, and great fun. (📞0131-225 5748; www.thevoyageofbuckedinburgh.co.uk; 29-31 William St; ⏱10am-midnight Mon-Wed, to 1am Thu-Sun; 🛜🐾; 🚇West End)

Blue Blazer
PUB

14 🍺 MAP P114, F4

With its mosaic floors, polished gantry, cosy fireplace and efficient bar staff, the Blue Blazer is a down-to-earth antidote to the designer excess of modern-style bars, catering to a loyal clientele of real-ale enthusiasts, rum aficionados (it's a venue for the Edinburgh Rum Club) and Saturday horseracing fans. (📞0131-229 5030; www.facebook.com/blueblazeredin; 2 Spittal St; ⏱11am-1am Mon-Sat, 12.30pm-1am Sun; 🛜; 🚌2, 300)

Indigo Yard
BAR

15 🍺 MAP P114, E2

Set around an airy, stone-floored and glass-roofed courtyard, Indigo Yard is a fashionable West End watering hole that has been patronised by the likes of Liam Gallagher, Pierce Brosnan and Kylie Minogue. Good food – including open-air barbecues during the summer months – just adds to the attraction. (📞0131-220 5603; www.indigoyardedinburgh.co.uk; 7 Charlotte Lane; ⏱8am-1am; 🛜👫; 🚌19, 36, 37, 41, 47)

Ghillie Dhu
PUB

16 🍺 MAP P114, E2

This spectacular bar, with its huge, chunky beer-hall tables, leather-sofa booths and polished black-and-white tile floor, makes a grand setting for the live folk-music sessions that take place here every night (from 10pm, admission free). (📞0131-222 9930; www.ghillie-dhu.co.uk; 2 Rutland Pl; ⏱11am-3am Mon-Fri, 10am-3am Sat & Sun; 🚌all Princes St buses)

Sygn

COCKTAIL BAR

17 🍸 MAP P114, E2

The plush banquettes and sleek, polished tables in this sharply styled bar are just the place to pose with a passionfruit bellini or a glass of Pol Roger. The languid and laid-back atmosphere is complemented by cool tunes and superb cocktails, and the food menu is surprisingly good. (📞0131-225 6060; www.sygn.co.uk; 15 Charlotte Lane; ⏱noon-1am; 📶; 🚌19, 36, 37, 41, 47)

Entertainment

Filmhouse

CINEMA

18 ⭐ MAP P114, E4

The Filmhouse is the main venue for the annual **Edinburgh International Film Festival** (📞0131-623 8030; www.edfilmfest.org.uk; ⏱Jun) and screens a full program of art-house, classic, foreign and second-run films, with lots of themes, retrospectives and 70mm screenings. It has wheelchair access to all three screens. (📞0131-228 2688; www.filmhousecinema.com; 88 Lothian Rd; 📶; 🚌all Lothian Rd buses)

West End cafes

West End Shops

Edinburgh's West End has a string of high-street chain stores on the main drag of Shandwick Pl, but there's also a hidden enclave of decadent designer shops clustered around the junction of William and Stafford Sts, plus the weekly food fest at the Edinburgh Farmers Market.

Henry's Cellar Bar
LIVE MUSIC

19 ⭐ MAP P114, E4

One of Edinburgh's most eclectic live-music venues, Henry's has something going on most nights of the week, from rock and indie to 'Balkan-inspired folk' and from funk and hip-hop to hardcore, staging both local bands and acts from around the world. (☎0131-629 2992; www.facebook.com/Henrys cellarbar; 16 Morrison St; free-£10; ⏰9pm-3am Sun & Tue-Thu, 8pm-3am Mon, 7pm-3am Fri & Sat; ☒all Lothian Rd buses)

Traverse Theatre
THEATRE

20 ⭐ MAP P114, F3

The Traverse is the main focus for new Scottish writing; it stages an adventurous program of contemporary drama and dance. The box office is only open on Sunday (from 4pm) when there's a show on. (☎0131-228 1404; www.traverse.co.uk; 10 Cambridge St; ⏰box office 10am-6pm Mon-Sat, to 7pm show nights; 📶; ☒all Lothian Rd buses)

Royal Lyceum Theatre
THEATRE

21 ⭐ MAP P114, F3

A grand Victorian theatre located beside the Usher Hall, the Lyceum stages drama, concerts, musicals and ballet. (☎0131-248 4848; www.lyceum.org.uk; 30b Grindlay St; ⏰box office 10am-5pm Mon-Sat, to 7pm show nights; ♿; ☒all Lothian Rd buses)

Usher Hall
CLASSICAL MUSIC

22 ⭐ MAP P114, E3

The architecturally impressive Usher Hall hosts concerts by the Royal Scottish National Orchestra (RSNO) and performances of popular music. (☎0131-228 1155; www.usherhall.co.uk; Lothian Rd; ⏰box office 10am-5.30pm, to 8pm show nights; ☒all Lothian Rd buses)

Murrayfield Stadium
STADIUM

23 ⭐ MAP P114, B4

Murrayfield Stadium, about 1.5 miles west of the city centre, is the venue for international rugby matches. (www.scottishrugby.org; 112 Roseburn St; 🚃Murrayfield Stadium)

Shopping

Assai Records
MUSIC

24 🔒 MAP P114, F3

An independent music shop that specialises in vinyl (old, new and

Usher Hall

remastered), Assai also has its own record label that promotes new Scottish talent. As well as a huge selection of discs, the shop stocks record players, band T-shirts and other music merchandise. (📞0131-228 3943; www.assai.co.uk; 1 Grindlay St; ⏰9.30am-6pm Mon & Wed-Sat, 10am-6pm Tue, noon-5pm Sun; 🚌2, 300)

Liam Ross   JEWELLERY

25 🔒 MAP P114, D2

Distinctive, hand-crafted jewellery is the hallmark of goldsmith Liam Ross. Choose from the range of gorgeous rings, bracelets and pendants on display, or commission a bespoke item from the man himself. (📞0131-225 6599; www.jewellerybyliamross.com; 12 William St; ⏰9am-5.30pm Tue-Fri, 10am-5pm Sat; 🚌West End)

Wonderland   TOYS

26 🔒 MAP P114, E4

Wonderland is a classic kids-with-their-noses-pressed-against-the-window toy shop that is filled with model aircraft, Lego *Star Wars* kits, radio-controlled cars and all sorts of other desirable things, but it also caters to the serious train-set and model-making fraternity. (📞0131-229 6428; www.wonderlandmodels.com; 97-101 Lothian Rd; ⏰9.30am-6pm Mon-Fri, 9am-6pm Sat; 🚌all Lothian Rd buses)

Explore
Stockbridge

Stockbridge is a bohemian enclave to the north of the city centre, with an interesting selection of shops and a good choice of pubs and neighbourhood bistros. Originally a mill village, it was developed in the early 19th century on lands owned largely by painter Sir Henry Raeburn, who gave his name to its main street, Raeburn Pl.

The best way to arrive in Stockbridge is by walking along the Water of Leith, starting from either Dean Village (10 minutes) or the Scottish National Gallery of Modern Art (25 minutes). Spend an hour browsing the shops on Raeburn Pl and St Stephen St before walking along the cobbled lane of St Bernard's Row, then Arboretum Ave and Arboretum Pl to the Royal Botanic Garden (p124), and plan to allow a couple of hours exploring its many attractions. Don't forget to grab a coffee at the garden's Terrace Cafe (p125) and soak up the view of the castle.

Getting There & Around

🚌 Lothian Buses 24, 29 and 42 run from Frederick St in the city centre to Raeburn Pl in Stockbridge. Bus 36 cuts across the neighbourhood from St Bernard's Cres and Leslie Pl to Hamilton Pl and Henderson Row.

Neighbourhood Map on p128

Stockbridge Market (p132) IAIN MASTERSTON/ALAMY ©

Top Sight 📷
Royal Botanic Garden

Edinburgh's Royal Botanic Garden is the second-oldest institution of its kind in Britain (after Oxford's), and one of the most respected in the world. Founded near Holyrood in 1670 and moved to its present location in 1823, it has 70 beautifully landscaped acres that include splendid Victorian glasshouses, colourful swaths of rhododendron and azalea, and a world-famous rock garden.

◎ MAP P128, C1

📞 0131-248 2909

www.rbge.org.uk

Arboretum Pl

admission free

🕐 10am-6pm Mar-Sep, to 5pm Feb & Oct, to 4pm Nov-Jan

🚌 8, 23, 27

John Hope Gateway

The garden's visitor centre is housed in this striking, environmentally friendly building overlooking the main Arboretum Pl entrance. There are exhibitions on biodiversity, climate change and sustainable development, as well as displays of rare plants from the institution's collection and a specially created biodiversity garden.

Glasshouses

A cluster of around 25 glasshouses in the garden's northern corner houses a huge collection of tropical plants. Pride of place goes to the ornate Victorian palm house (pictured left), built in 1834 and home to vast rainforest palms, including a Bermudan palmetto that dates from 1822. The Front Range of 1960s designer glasshouses is famous for its tropical pond filled with giant Amazonian water lilies.

Rock Garden

Since it was first created in 1871 the rock garden has been one of the garden's most popular features. Boulders and scree slopes made from Scottish sandstone and conglomerate are home to more than 4000 species of alpine and subarctic plants from all over the world.

Sculptures

Pick up a map from the visitor centre so that you can track down the garden's numerous sculptures, ranging from a statue of Swedish botanist and taxonomist Carl Linnaeus (1707–78) by Scottish architect Robert Adam, to modern works by Yorkshire sculptor Barbara Hepworth and landscape artist Andy Goldsworthy.

★ Top Tips

o Guided tours of the gardens (£6 per person) depart at 11am and 2pm daily from April to October.

o The main entrance is the West Gate on Arboretum Pl, where the Majestic Tour bus drops off and picks up; however, city buses stop near the smaller East Gate on Inverleith Row.

o It's worth consulting the website before your visit to check out what the current month's seasonal highlights are.

✗ Take a Break

The Gateway Restaurant (p127) in the John Hope Gateway visitor centre serves hot breakfast and lunch dishes.

The **Terrace Cafe** (☎ 0131-552 0606; Royal Botanic Garden, Arboretum Pl; mains £5-8; ⏱ 10.30am-5pm; 👶; 🚌 8, 23, 27), in the middle of the gardens, has outdoor tables with a superb view of the city skyline.

Walking Tour 🚶‍♂️

A Sunday Stroll Around Stockbridge

Just a short walk downhill from the city centre, Stockbridge feels a world away with its peaceful backstreets, leafy Georgian gardens, quirky boutiques and art galleries, and the Water of Leith flowing through the middle. There's a strong community spirit that really comes alive on Sunday, when Stockbridge Market attracts crowds of local shoppers and browsers.

Walk Facts

Start Gateway Restaurant

End Stockbridge Market

Length Two miles; 1.5 hours

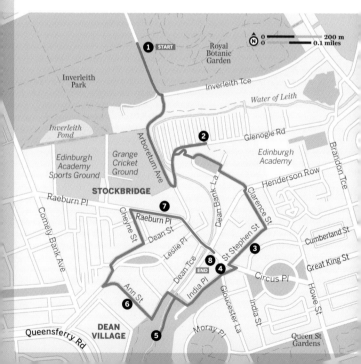

❶ Breakfast at the Botanics

Take bus 8, 23 or 27 to the main entrance to the Royal Botanic Garden on Arboretum Pl, and head for the **Gateway Restaurant** (☎0131-552 2674; John Hope Gateway, Royal Botanic Garden, Arboretum Pl; mains £8-10; ☺10am-6pm Mar-Sep, to 5pm Feb & Oct, to 4pm Nov-Jan; 🚸; 🚌8, 23, 27) to enjoy breakfast with a view over the gardens.

❷ Stockbridge Colonies

A short walk along Arboretum Pl and Arboretum Ave leads to the Stockbridge Colonies, a series of terraced stone houses built by a workers' co-operative in the 19th century to provide affordable working-class accommodation (now not so affordable). Carved stone plaques on several gable ends show the tools of the tradesmen who built them.

❸ Browse St Stephen Street's shops

This side street is pure Stockbridge, crammed with tiny galleries, boutiques, restaurants and basement bars. **Miss Bizio** (www.missbiziocouture.com) is a cornucopia of high-end vintage fashion, while **Sheila Fleet** (https://sheila fleet.com) is a showcase for the work of the Orkney-based jewellery designer. At St Stephen Pl, you can see the Georgian archway that once led to the old Stockbridge meat market.

❹ Gloucester Lane

This steep, cobbled street was once the main thoroughfare connecting Stockbridge to the city, before the New Town was built. **Duncan's Land**, at the corner with India Pl – now **Nok's Kitchen** (p131) – is one of Stockbridge's oldest surviving buildings, dating from 1790, though it used masonry from demolished Old Town buildings (the lintel is dated 1605).

❺ St Bernard's Well

A short walk along the Water of Leith Walkway leads to **St Bernard's Well** (p129). The sulphurous spring was discovered by schoolboys from **George Heriot's School** (p47) in 1760.

❻ Ann Street

The Georgian garden villas along Ann St (named after Sir Henry Raeburn's wife; 1817) are among the most beautiful and desirable houses in Edinburgh – the street is reckoned to be the most expensive in the city, and was named in 2008 as one of the UK's six most exclusive streets. It is also the setting for JM Barrie's 1902 novel *Quality Street*.

❼ Raeburn Place

Stockbridge's main drag is a bustle of shops, pubs and restaurants, with everything from chain stores and charity shops to craft shops, galleries and jewellery boutiques.

❽ Stockbridge Market

On Sunday, **Stockbridge Market** (p132) is the focus of the community, set in a leafy square next to the bridge that gives the district its name.

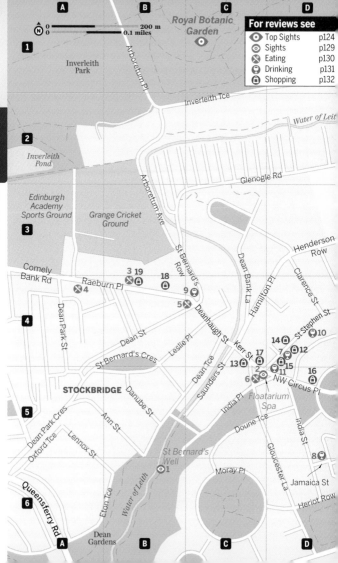

For reviews see

⊙	Top Sights	p124
⊙	Sights	p129
⊗	Eating	p130
⊟	Drinking	p131
⊡	Shopping	p132

Inverleith Park

Inverleith Tce

Water of Leith

Inverleith Pond

Glenogle Rd

Edinburgh Academy Sports Ground

Grange Cricket Ground

Henderson Row

Comely Bank Rd

Raeburn Pl

Dean Bank La

Clarence St

St Stephen St

3 19
⊗ ⊡

⊗ 4

18
⊡

9 ⊡

5 ⊗

14 ⊡   ⊗ 10

Dean St

Leslie Pl

Kerr St

17 ⊡   7 ⊡ 12

Dean Park St

St Bernard's Cres

Dean Tce

13 ⊡   11 ⊡ 15

Danube St

Saunders St

2
6 ⊗⊙   NW Circus Pl

16 ⊡

STOCKBRIDGE

Ann St

India Pl

Floatarium Spa

Doune Tce

Dean Park Cres

Oxford Tce

Lennox St

Eton Tce

St Bernard's Well

Moray Pl

Gloucester La

8 ⊟

Queensferry Rd

Water of Leith

⊙ 1

India St

Jamaica St

Heriot Row

Dean Gardens

A   B   C   D

Sights

St Bernard's Well

MONUMENT

1 MAP P128, B6

St Bernard's Well is a circular temple with a statue of Hygeia, the goddess of health, built in 1789. The sulphurous spring within was discovered by schoolboys from George Heriot's School in 1760, and became hugely popular during the late-18th-century fad for 'taking the waters' – one visitor compared the taste to 'the washings of foul gun barrels'. (Water of Leith Walkway; admission free; ☉noon-3pm first Sun of month Apr-Aug; 🚌24, 29, 36, 42)

Floatarium Spa

SPA

2 MAP P128, C5

Escape from the bustle of the city centre in a warm, womb-like flotation tank, or enjoy the many other therapies on offer, including facials, aromatherapy massage, reflexology, shiatsu, reiki and Indian head massage (appointments necessary). There's a sweet-scented shop, too, where you can buy massage oils, incense, candles, homeopathic remedies and CDs. (📞0131-225 3350; https:// edinburghfloatarium.co.uk; 29 NW Circus Pl; 1hr treatment from £45; ☉10am-3pm Mon, to 8pm Tue-Fri, to 6pm Sat, to 5pm Sun; 🚌24, 29, 42)

St Bernard's Well

Water of Leith

Edinburgh's river is a modest stream, flowing only 20 miles from the northwestern slopes of the Pentland Hills to enter the Firth of Forth at Leith. It cuts a surprisingly rural swath through the city, providing an important wildlife habitat (you can occasionally see otters and kingfishers) and offering the chance to stroll along wooded river-banks only 500m from Princes St. The **Water of Leith Walkway** offers an almost uninterrupted 12-mile walking and cycling route along the river from Leith via Stockbridge and Dean Village to Balerno, on the southwestern edge of the city.

Eating

Henri of Edinburgh DELI £

3 🍴 MAP P128, B4

This spacious French deli-cafe supplies many of Edinburgh's top restaurants, and boasts some of the best cheese and charcuterie the city has to offer. It's popular with locals, families and Franco-philes, and the sandwiches are exceptional, as are the wine, coffee and hot chocolate. Opens as a wine bar on Thursday, Friday and Saturday from 6pm. (📞0131-332 8963; www.henriofedinburgh.com; 48 Raeburn Pl; mains £8-11; ⏱9am-7pm Mon-Wed, to 11pm Thu-Sat, 10am-6.30pm Sun; 👶; 🚌24, 29, 42)

Scran & Scallie GASTROPUB ££

4 🍴 MAP P128, A4

Established by the Michelin-starred team responsible for Kitch-in (p140) and Castle Terrace (p115), this laid-back gastropub adds a modern chef's touch to old-time dishes such as chicken-liver parfait, sausage and mash, and steak pie. There are also quality versions of classic pub grub such as burgers, seafood pie, and fish and chips, and veggie options that include a beetroot-and-lentil burger. (📞0131-332 6281; https://scranandscallie.com; 1 Comely Bank Rd; mains £12-20; ⏱noon-10pm Mon-Fri, 8.30-10pm Sat & Sun; 📶👶🎒; 🚌24, 29, 42)

Taisteal INTERNATIONAL

5 🍴 MAP P128, C4

Taisteal is the Gaelic word for 'travel', so it's no surprise that the menu in this convivial bistro is a fusion of Scottish produce with influences and flavours from around the world – rabbit and pancetta ballotine with rabbit haggis and wild-garlic gnocchi is a typical concoction. There's also a three-course lunch for £16, and a five-course tasting menu for £35. (📞0131-332 9977; www.taisteal.co.uk; 1-3 Raeburn Pl; mains £14-19; ⏱noon-2.30pm & 6-9.30pm Tue-Sat; 🚌24, 29, 36, 42)

Nok's Kitchen

THAI ££

6 ⊗ MAP P128, C5

Nok's dishes up a menu of authentic and beautifully presented Thai food in the romantic atmosphere of a 17th-century town house, decorated with Thai paintings, statues and woodcarvings. Two-course lunch for £9.95. (☎ 0131-225 4804; www.nokskitchen.co.uk; 8 Gloucester St; mains £9-18; ⊙ noon-2.30pm & 5.30-10pm; ☒ 24, 29, 42)

Drinking

Last Word Saloon

COCKTAIL BAR

7 ⊕ MAP P128, D4

This cosy, dimly lit basement bar is unpretentious and just a little bit grungy. The cocktails are outstanding, with an extensive list including the complex Lear's Lyric (Hendrick's gin, ABA Pisco, manzanilla sherry, avocado leaf, lemon, sugarsnap-pea syrup and celery bitters), and a small but interesting whisky menu – a good place to start exploring single malts. (☎ 0131-225 9009; www.lastwordsaloon.com; 44 St Stephen St; ⊙ 4pm-1am; ☒ 24, 29, 42)

Kay's Bar

PUB

8 ⊕ MAP P128, D5

Housed in a former wine merchant's office, tiny Kay's is a cosy haven with a coal fire and a fine range of real ales. Good food is served in the back room at lunchtime, but you'll have to book a table – it's a popular spot.

(☎ 0131-225 1858; www.kaysbar.co.uk; 39 Jamaica St; ⊙ 11am-midnight Mon-Thu, to 1am Fri & Sat, 12.30-11pm Sun; ☜; ☒ 24, 29, 42)

Stockbridge Tap

PUB

9 ⊕ MAP P128, C4

This cosy bar has more of a lounge atmosphere (sofas at the back) than a traditional Edinburgh pub, but the counter reveals that it is dedicated to real ale – there are seven hand-pulled pints on offer, with three house and four guest beers. Good range of craft gins, too. (☎ 0131-343 3000; www.facebook.com/thestockbridgetap; 2 Raeburn Pl; ⊙ noon-midnight Mon-Thu, to 1am Fri & Sat, 12.30pm-midnight Sun; ☜ ☻; ☒ 24, 29, 36, 42)

Antiquary

PUB

10 ⊕ MAP P128, D4

A dark, downstairs den of traditional beersmanship, with bare wooden floorboards and dark wood tables and chairs, the long-established Antiquary has lively folk-music sessions from 8.30pm on Thursday, and Wednesday quiz nights. (☎ 0131-225 2858; www.theantiquarybar.co.uk; 72-78 St Stephen St; ⊙ 4-11pm Mon, 4pm-midnight Tue, noon-midnight Wed, noon-1am Thu-Sat, 12.30pm-midnight Sun; ☒ 24, 29, 42)

Bailie Bar

PUB

11 ⊕ MAP P128, D5

Tucked in a basement, the Bailie is a Stockbridge stalwart – a dimly lit, warm and welcoming nook with a large circular island bar, a roaring fire in winter, and TVs screening live football. Serves good coffee as well as real ales and malt whiskies. (📞0131-225 4673; www.thebailiebar.com; 2 St Stephen St; ⏰11am-midnight Mon-Thu, to 1am Fri & Sat, 12.30pm-midnight Sun; 🚌24, 29, 42)

Shopping

Golden Hare Books   BOOKS

12 🔒 MAP P128, D4

Independent bookshops don't get lovelier than this. The Golden Hare boasts a great selection of 'beautiful, unusual and interesting books', an enchanting children's nook, and a small but perfectly formed events program. A must if you love books, book design and beautiful shops. (📞0131-629 1396; https://goldenharebooks.com; 68 St Stephen St; ⏰10am-6pm; 🚌24, 29, 42)

Stockbridge Market   MARKET

13 🔒 MAP P128, C4

On Sunday the local community's focus is Stockbridge Market, set in a leafy square next to the bridge that gives the district its name. Wares range from fresh Scottish produce to handmade ceramics, jewellery, soaps and cosmetics. Grab an espresso from Steampunk Coffee, which operates out of a 1970s VW campervan. (www.stockbridgemarket.com; cnr Kerr & Saunders Sts; ⏰10am-5pm Sun; 🚌24, 29, 36, 42)

Miss Bizio   VINTAGE

14 🔒 MAP P128, D4

Established by an enthusiast who has been collecting vintage fashion for more than 30 years, this boutique is a cornucopia of high-end clothes and accessories from the Victorian era to the 1970s. Not much in the way of bargains, but fascinating to browse through. (📞07775 583675; www.facebook.com/missbizio; 41 St Stephen St; ⏰11am-6pm Mon, Tue & Thu-Sat; 🚌24, 29, 42)

Sheila Fleet   JEWELLERY

15 🔒 MAP P128, D4

This Edinburgh gallery is a showcase for the work of Orkney-based designer Sheila Fleet, whose gold, silver and platinum jewellery is inspired by the colours and textures of her native island's landscapes. (📞0131-225 5939; https://sheilafleet.com; 18 St Stephen St; ⏰10am-5.30pm Mon-Sat; 🚌24, 29, 42)

Dick's   FASHION & ACCESSORIES

16 🔒 MAP P128, D5

Men's and women's fashion, accessories and homewares from independent manufacturers. (📞0131-226 6220; https://dicks-edinburgh.co.uk; 3 NW Circus Pl; ⏰11am-6pm Mon-Sat, noon-5pm Sun; 🚌24, 29, 42)

Ian Mellis   FOOD & DRINKS

17 🔒 MAP P128, C4

Stockbridge branch of the famous Old Town **cheese shop** (30a Victoria

Miss Bizio vintage shop

St; ⏰9.30am-7pm Mon-Sat, 11am-6pm Sun), selling traditional Scottish cheeses, from creamy Hebridean Blue to sweet and nutty Loch Arthur cheddar. Located off Kerr St. (☎0131-225 6566; www.mellischeese. co.uk; 6 Bakers Pl; ⏰9am-7pm Mon-Fri, 8.30am-6pm Sat, 10am-5.30pm Sun; 🚍24, 29, 42)

Annie Smith
JEWELLERY

18 🔒 MAP P128, B4

Annie Smith's back-of-the-shop studio creates beautiful and original contemporary jewellery in silver and 18-carat gold, with beaten and worked surfaces that reflect natural textures such as rock, ice and leaves. If there's

nothing in the shop that takes your fancy, you can commission Ms Smith to make something to order. (☎0131-332 5749; www.anniesmith. co.uk; 12 Raeburn Pl; ⏰10am-5.30pm Mon-Sat, noon-5pm Sun; 🚍24, 29, 42)

Galerie Mirages
JEWELLERY

19 🔒 MAP P128, B4

An Aladdin's cave packed with jewellery, textiles and handicrafts from all over the world, Mirages is best known for its silver, amber and gemstone jewellery in both culturally traditional and contemporary designs. (☎0131-315 2603; www.galeriemirages.com; 46a Raeburn Pl; ⏰10am-5.30pm Mon-Sat, 12-4.30pm Sun; 🚍24, 29, 42)

Explore ◈
Leith

Leith has been Edinburgh's seaport since the 14th century, but it fell into decay following WWII. It's now undergoing a steady revival, with old warehouses turned into luxury flats and a lush crop of trendy bars and restaurants sprouting along the waterfront leading to Ocean Terminal, a huge new shopping and leisure complex, and the former Royal Yacht Britannia.

The Royal Yacht Britannia (p136) is best visited first thing in the morning as soon as it opens at 9.30am; to avoid standing in line, you can buy tickets online until 4pm the previous day. After a morning exploring the ship, you can walk to The Shore (p139) and enjoy a slap-up seafood lunch at Fishers Bistro (p140) or Shore (p141). Spend the afternoon discovering the history of golf at Leith Links (p139), shopping for tartan at Kinloch Anderson (p144), and browsing the exhibitions at Edinburgh Sculpture Workshop (p139). In the evening, take your pick of Michelin-starred restaurants – Martin Wishart (p140) or Kitchin (p140).

Getting There & Around

🚌 Leith is well served by bus routes. Lothian Buses 12, 16 and 22 run from Princes St down Leith. Walk to the junction of Constitution and Great Junction Sts; from here 16 goes west to Newhaven; 22 goes north to The Shore and Ocean Terminal; and 12 goes east to Leith Links. Buses 200 and 300 link the airport to Ocean Terminal.

Neighbourhood Map on p138

Waterside in Leith RICHIE CHAN/SHUTTERSTOCK ©

Top Sight 📷
Royal Yacht Britannia

Built on Clydeside, the former Royal Yacht Britannia was the British royal family's floating holiday home during their foreign travels from the time of her launch in 1953 until her decommissioning in 1997. The ship is now permanently moored in front of Ocean Terminal, and a tour provides an intriguing insight into the Queen's private tastes.

◎ MAP P138, B2

www.royalyachtbritannia.
co.uk

Ocean Terminal

adult/child incl audioguide
£16/8.50

🕐 9.30am-6pm Apr-Sep,
to 5.30pm Oct, 10am-5pm
Nov-Mar, last entry 1½hr
before closing

🚌 11, 22, 34, 36, 200, 300

State Apartments

The *Britannia* is a monument to 1950s decor, and the accommodation reveals Her Majesty's preference for simple, unfussy surroundings. The Queen travelled with 45 members of the royal household, five tonnes of luggage and a Rolls-Royce that was squeezed into a specially built garage on the deck (it's still there). The **State Drawing Room**, which once hosted royal receptions, is furnished with chintz sofas bolted firmly to the floor, and a baby grand piano where Noël Coward once tickled the ivories.

Royal Bedrooms

The private cabins of the Queen and Prince Philip are surprisingly small and plain, with ordinary 3ft-wide single beds (the only double bed on board is in the honeymoon suite, used by Prince Charles and Princess Diana in 1981). The thermometer in the Queen's bathroom was used to make sure the water was the correct temperature.

On Deck

The decks (of Burmese teak) were scrubbed daily, but all work near the royal accommodation was carried out in complete silence and had to be finished by 8am. When the ship was in harbour one yachtsman was charged with ensuring that the angle of the gangway never exceeded 12 degrees. Note the mahogany windbreak that was added to the balcony deck in front of the bridge: it was put there to stop wayward breezes from blowing up skirts and inadvertently revealing the royal undies.

Bloodhound

Britannia was joined in 2010 by the 1930s racing yacht *Bloodhound,* which was owned by the Queen in the 1960s. *Bloodhound* is moored alongside *Britannia* (except in July and August, when she is away cruising) as part of an exhibition about the royal family's love of all things nautical.

★ **Top Tips**

o You tour the ship at your own pace, using an audioguide. You'll need at least two hours to see everything.

o The **Majestic Tour** (p139) bus runs from Waverley Bridge to *Britannia* during the ship's opening times.

o The Royal Edinburgh Ticket, available from Majestic Tour, covers admission to *Britannia*, Edinburgh Castle and the Palace of Holyroodhouse, plus two days' travel on local tour buses.

✗ **Take a Break**

Britannia's sun deck (now enclosed in glass) makes a stunning setting for the **Royal Deck Tea Room** (www.royalyachtbritannia.co.uk; Ocean Terminal; mains £6-14; ⏱10am-4.30pm Apr-Oct, 10.30am-4pm Nov-Mar; 🚌11, 22, 34, 36, 200, 300), where you can enjoy coffee and cake, or even a bottle of champagne, with a view across the Firth of Forth to the hills of Fife.

Leith

N

0   200 m
0   0.1 miles

Western
Harbour

**Royal Yacht
Britannia**
◉

Leith
Docks

Imperial
Dock

24🔒

Ocean Dr

Ocean Dr

Ocean Dr

Ocean Dr

Victoria
Dock

Albert
Dock

◉3

Lindsay Rd

Victoria Quay

Commercial Quay

Commercial St

Lindsay St

N Junction St

13 7
✗✗

Dock Pl

🔒21

20

Tower Pl

5
🍷

Tower St

Portland St

Madeira St

1◉ The Shore
9 → Timber
17 Bush

N Fort St

Coburg St

Sandport Pl

14✗

Water of Leith

🍷22

Bernard St

Ferry Rd

Mill La

Sheriff Brae

16
🍷

The Shore

6
✗

Water St

18
🍷

Maritime St

Baltic S

19
🍷

Mitchell St

✗10

Pitt St

Cables Wynd

Tolbooth
Wynd

Giles St

Kirkgate

Queen
Charlotte St

Mitchell St

11🍷

Links

W Bowling Green St

Bangor Rd

Great Junction St

Henderson St

Wellington Pl

John's Pl

Constitution St

Duncan Pl

2
🔒
Leith
Link

🍷 Biscuit
Factory 4
🔒

Bonnington Rd

Tennant St

Jane St

15🍷

Duke St

Hermitage

Anderson Pl

Pilrig
Park

Pilrig St

Balfour St

Leith Walk

Gordon St

Halmyre St

Easter Rd

Lochend Rd

8 12 23
✗✗🔒

Sights

The Shore
AREA

1 MAP P138, C3

The most attractive part of Leith is this cobbled waterfront street alongside the Water of Leith, lined with pubs and restaurants. Before the docks were built in the 19th century this was Leith's original wharf. An iron plaque in front of No 30 marks the King's Landing – the spot where George IV (the first reigning British monarch to visit Scotland since Charles II in 1650) stepped ashore in 1822. (🚌16, 22, 36, 300)

Leith Links
PARK

2 MAP P138, D5

This public park was originally common grazing land but is more famous as the birthplace of modern golf. Although St Andrews has the oldest golf course in the world, it was at Leith Links in 1744 that the first official rules of the game were formulated by the Honourable Company of Edinburgh Golfers. A stone cairn on the western side of the park bears a plaque describing how the ancient game was played over five holes of around 400yd each. (🚌12, 21, 25, 34, 49)

Edinburgh Sculpture Workshop
ARTS CENTRE

3 🔵 MAP P138, A2

This state-of-the-art building located on an old railway siding is the first purpose-built centre

The Majestic Tour

Hop-on, hop-off **tour** (www.edinburghtour.com; adult/child £15/7.50; ⊙daily year-round except 25 Dec) departing every 15 to 20 minutes from Waverley Bridge to the Royal Yacht *Britannia* at Ocean Terminal via the New Town, the Royal Botanic Garden and Newhaven, returning via Leith Walk, Holyrood and the Royal Mile.

dedicated to sculpture in the UK. There are regular exhibitions, talks and courses. Combine a visit with lunch at the top-notch on-site cafe run by Edinburgh's Milk and a stroll along the Hawthornvale path, which connects to the Water of Leith walkway. (📞0131-551 4490; www.edinburghsculpture.org; 21 Hawthornvale; admission free; ⊙9.30am-5pm Mon-Sat; 🅿; 🚌7, 11)

Biscuit Factory
ARTS CENTRE

4 🔵 MAP P138, A5

This recent addition to Leith's hipster scene is a creative arts hub housed in an old biscuit factory, also home to Edinburgh Gin's second distillery. Events range from food markets to random club nights. It's still early days, but other plans include creating 20 studios over two floors, a cafe and bar, and a community garden on the roof. (📞0131-629 0809; www.biscuitfactory.co.uk; 4-6 Anderson Pl; ⊙10am-5pm; 🚌11, 36)

Eating

Fishers Bistro

SEAFOOD ££

5 🍴 MAP P138, D3

This cosy little restaurant, tucked beneath a 17th-century signal tower, is one of the city's best seafood places. The menu ranges widely in price, from cheaper dishes such as classic fish cakes with lemon-and-chive mayonnaise to more expensive delights such as Fife lobster and chips (£40). (📞 0131-554 5666; www.fishersbistros.co.uk; 1 The Shore; mains £14-25; ⏲ noon-10.30pm Mon-Sat, 12.30-10.30pm Sun; 📶🍴👪; 🚌 16, 22, 36, 300)

Martin Wishart

FRENCH £££

6 🍴 MAP P138, C4

In 2001 this restaurant became the first in Edinburgh to win a Michelin star, and it's retained it ever since. The eponymous chef has worked with Albert Roux, Marco Pierre White and Nick Nairn, and brings a modern French approach to the best Scottish produce, from langoustines with white asparagus and confit onion to a six-course vegetarian tasting menu (£75). (📞 0131-553 3557; www. martin-wishart.co.uk; 54 The Shore; 3-course lunch £32, 4-course dinner £90; ⏲ noon-2pm & 7-10pm Tue-Fri, noon-1.30pm & 7-10pm Sat; 🍴; 🚌 16, 22, 36, 300)

Kitchin

SCOTTISH £££

7 🍴 MAP P138, C3

Fresh, seasonal, locally sourced Scottish produce is the philosophy that has won a Michelin star for this elegant but unpretentious restaurant. The menu moves with the seasons, of course, so expect fresh salads in summer and game in winter, and shellfish dishes such as baked scallops with white wine, vermouth and herb sauce when there's an 'r' in the month. (📞 0131-555 1755; http://thekitchin.com; 78 Commercial Quay; 3-course lunch/dinner £33/75; ⏲ noon-2.30pm & 6-10pm Tue-Sat; 🍴; 🚌 16, 22, 36, 300)

Twelve Triangles

BAKERY £

8 🍴 MAP P138, B6

Tucked away on an unassuming stretch just off Leith Walk, Twelve Triangles is an exceptional (and exceptionally tiny) bakery. Some of the city's best artisan breads, pastries and coffee come out of its clever kitchen, and the doughnut fillings are legendary, encompassing pistachio custard, pink-grapefruit ricotta, and chocolate and peanut butter. Coffee and doughnuts don't get more sophisticated. (📞 0131-629 4664; www.twelvetriangles.com; 90 Brunswick St; mains £2-3; ⏲ 8am-5pm Mon-Fri, 9am-5pm Sat & Sun; 🚌 all Leith Walk buses)

Cramond

Originally a mill village, Cramond has a historic 17th-century church and a 15th-century tower house, as well as some rather unimpressive Roman remains, but most people come to enjoy the walks along the river to the ruined mills and to stroll along the seafront. On the riverside, opposite the cottage on the far bank, is the Maltings, which hosts an interesting exhibition on Cramond's history. With its moored yachts, stately swans and whitewashed houses spilling down the hillside at the mouth of the River Almond, Cramond is the most picturesque corner of Edinburgh.

Shore   SEAFOOD ££

9 🍽 MAP P138, C3

The atmospheric dining room in the popular Shore pub is a haven of wood-panelled peace, with old photographs, nautical knick-knacks, fresh flowers and an open fire adding to the romantic theme. The menu changes regularly and specialises in fresh Scottish seafood, beef, pork and game. (📞0131-553 5080; www.fishersrestaurants.co.uk; 3-4 The Shore; mains £14-20; ⏱noon-10.30pm Mon-Sat, 12.30-10.30pm Sun; 🛜👶; 🚌16, 22, 36, 300)

Pitt   MARKET £

10 🍽 MAP P138, A4

A weekly street-food market surrounded by industrial warehouses, The Pitt is a little bit of East London in north Edinburgh. The regularly changing food trucks sell anything from burgers stuffed with crab to halloumi bao buns to haggis to sweet-potato pierogis.

Choose a drink from the wine and gin bars, or the Barneys beer truck selling local craft ales. (📞07736 281893; www.thepitt.co.uk; 125 Pitt St; entry £2; ⏱noon-10pm Sat Mar-Dec; 🚌7, 11, 14)

Chop House Leith   STEAK £££

11 🍽 MAP P138, D4

A modern take on the old-fashioned steakhouse, this 'bar and butchery' combines slick designer decor (the ceramic brick tiles are a nod to traditional butcher shops) with a meaty menu of the best Scottish beef, dry-aged for at least 35 days and chargrilled to perfection. Sauces include bone-marrow gravy and Argentine chimichurri. Cool cocktails, too. (📞0131-629 1919; www.chophouse steak.co.uk; 102 Constitution St; mains £17-29; ⏱noon-3pm & 5-10.30pm Mon-Fri, 10am-10.30pm Sat & Sun; 🛜; 🚌12, 16)

Serrano & Manc29ego TAPAS ££

12  MAP P138, C6

This relaxed and informal tapas bar imports the eponymous ham and cheese direct from Spain, along with other Iberian goodies such as Padrón peppers, Bellota chorizo and Gallega octopus. Sit down to a mixed platter of Spanish cheese and charcuterie washed down with a refreshing glass of *albariño*. (📞 0131-554 0955; http://serranoandmanchego.co.uk; ⏰ 9am-1am; 🚌 all Leith Walk buses)

Quay Commons CAFE £

13 MAP P138, C3

A combined deli, bakery and licensed cafe run by the same people behind Gardener's Cottage (p100), this is a designer conversion of a former bonded warehouse where you can watch the bakers at work. It serves healthy soups, sandwiches and salads at lunch, plus handmade pasta dishes on Friday and Saturday evening. (📞 0131-677 0244; www.quaycommons.co; 92 Commercial Quay; mains £6-12; ⏰ 8am-6pm Mon-Thu, to 10pm Fri & Sat, 9am-6pm Sun; 📶; 🚌 16, 22, 36, 300)

Drinking

Roseleaf BAR

14 MAP P138, C3

Cute, quaint, and decked out in flowered wallpaper, old furniture and rose-patterned china (cocktails are served in teapots), the Roseleaf could hardly be

Fishers Bistro (p140)

Meals & Brews in Leith

🍽

Leith is renowned for its clutch of excellent restaurants, including two with Michelin stars Martin Wishart (p140) the Kitchin (p140), as well as lots of good-value bistros and pubs, many with outdoor seating and river views in summer.

With its long history as a dockyard neighbourhood, it's not surprising that Leith has more than its fair share of historic pubs, including Carriers Quarters and Port O'Leith (p144), plus newer ones housed in historic buildings, such as Teuchters Landing (p144). Plenty of modern bars like Sofi's and the Roseleaf have sprung up as well, catering to the inhabitants of newly developed apartment blocks and offices.

further from the average Leith bar. The real ales and bottled beers are complemented by a range of speciality teas, coffees and fruit drinks (including rose lemonade), and well-above-average pub grub (served from 10am to 10pm). (☎0131-476 5268; www.roseleaf.co.uk; 23-24 Sandport Pl; ⏰10am-1am; 📶👶; 🚌16, 22, 36, 300)

Lioness of Leith

BAR

15 🚇 MAP P138, C5

Duke St was always one of the rougher corners of Leith, but the emergence of pubs like the Lioness is a sure sign of gentrification. Distressed timber and battered leather benches are surrounded by vintage *objets trouvés,* a pinball machine and a pop-art print of Allen Ginsberg. Good beers and cocktails, and a tempting menu of gourmet burgers. (☎0131-629 0580; www.thelionessofleith.co.uk; 21-25 Duke St; ⏰noon-1am Mon-Thu,

11am-1am Fri-Sun; 📶; 🚌21, 25, 34, 49, 300)

Sofi's

BAR

16 🚇 MAP P138, C4

Sofi's brings a little bit of Swedish sophistication to this former Leith pub, feeling more like a bohemian cafe with its mismatched furniture, candlelit tables, fresh flowers and colourful art. It's a real community place, too, hosting film screenings, book clubs, open-mic music nights, and even a knitting club! (☎0131-555 7019; www.bodabar.com/sofis; 65 Henderson St; ⏰2pm-1am Mon-Fri, noon-1am Sat, 1pm-1am Sun; 📶👶; 🚌22, 36, 300)

Carriers Quarters

PUB

17 🚇 MAP P138, D3

With a low wooden ceiling, stone walls and a fine old fireplace, the Carriers has all the historic atmosphere that its 18th-century origins would imply. It serves real ales and malt whiskies, as well as traditional Scottish bar meals such as pies, stovies (meat and potato dish) and haggis. (☎0131-554 4122; www. carriersquarters.co.uk; 42 Bernard St; ◷noon-1am; 🐾; 🚌16, 22, 36, 300)

Nobles
PUB

18 🚇 MAP P138, D4

In an area stuffed with choice pubs, Nobles might be the most loved by locals. This beautifully restored Victorian cafe-bar in the heart of Leith has original stained-glass windows, wood panelling and a nautical theme that speaks to the history of this old port. The food is straightforward and modestly priced and the choice of ales excellent. (☎0131-629 7215; http://new.noblesbarleith.co.uk; 44a Constitution St; ◷10am-11pm Tue, Wed & Sun, to midnight Thu, to 1am Fri & Sat; 🚌12, 16)

Port O'Leith
PUB

19 🚇 MAP P138, D4

This good old-fashioned local boozer has been sympathetically restored – it appeared in the 2013 film *Sunshine on Leith*. Its nautical history is evident in the form of flags and cap bands left behind by visiting sailors (Leith docks are just down the road). Pop in for a pint and you'll probably stay until closing time. (☎0131-554 3568; www.facebook.com/ThePortOLeithBar; 58 Constitution St; ◷11am-1am Mon-Sat, noon-1am Sun; 🚌12, 16)

Teuchters Landing
PUB

20 🚇 MAP P138, C3

A cosy warren of timber-lined nooks and crannies housed in a single-storey red-brick building (once a waiting room for ferries across the Firth of Forth), this real-ale and malt-whisky bar also has tables on a floating terrace in the dock. (☎0131-554 7427; www. aroomin.co.uk; 1 Dock Pl; ◷10.30am-1am; 📶; 🚌16, 22, 36, 300)

Shopping

Kinloch Anderson
FASHION & ACCESSORIES

21 🔒 MAP P138, C3

One of the best tartan shops in Edinburgh, Kinloch Anderson was founded in 1868 and is still family run. It is a supplier of kilts and Highland dress to the royal family. (☎0131-555 1390; www.kinloch anderson.com; 4 Dock St; ◷9am-5.30pm Mon-Sat; 🚌16, 22, 36, 300)

Flux
ARTS & CRAFTS

22 🔒 MAP P138, C3

Flux is an outlet for contemporary British and overseas arts and crafts, including stained glass, metalware, jewellery and ceramics, all ethically sourced and much of it made using recycled materials. (☎0131-554 4075; www.get2flux. co.uk; 55 Bernard St; ◷10.30am-6pm Mon-Sat, noon-5pm Sun; 🚌16, 22, 36, 300)

Ocean Terminal

Flea Market

MARKET

23 MAP P138, C6

A Paris-style flea market it ain't, but this monthly rummage through the back of Leith's collective cupboards is an interesting place to trawl for vintage clothes and accessories, old books, tools, toys and scratched vinyl. (http://edinburghfleamarket.blogspot.co.uk; Drill Hall, 36 Dalmeny St; ⏱10am-3pm last Sat of month; 🛜♿; 🚌all Leith Walk buses)

Ocean Terminal

MALL

24 MAP P138, B2

Anchored by Debenhams department store, Ocean Terminal is the biggest shopping centre in Edinburgh; fashion outlets include Fat Face, GAP, Schuh, Superdry and White Stuff. The complex also includes access to the former Royal Yacht *Britannia* and a berth for visiting cruise liners. (📞0131-555 8888; www.oceanterminal.com; Ocean Dr; ⏱10am-8pm Mon-Fri, to 7pm Sat, 11am-6pm Sun; 🛜; 🚌11, 22, 34, 36, 200, 300)

Explore
South Edinburgh

Stretching south from the Old Town and taking in the 19th-century tenements of Tollcross, Bruntsfield, Marchmont and Sciennes (pronounced 'sheens'), and the upmarket suburbs of Newington, Grange and Morningside, this is a peaceful residential neighbourhood of smart Victorian flats and spacious garden villas. There's not much by way of tourist attractions, but there are many good restaurants, cafes and pubs.

Start with a stroll through The Meadows (p150) – there might be a cricket match on – and spend the rest of the morning browsing the exhibits at Summerhall (p150) and/or visiting the Surgeons' Hall Museums (p150). After lunch at Field Southside (p152), take a bus to Blackford Hill (p151). Climb to the summit for a glorious view across the city to the castle, the Old Town skyline and Arthur's Seat. Book well in advance for dinner at Aizle (p151), and a show at the Festival Theatre (p157). If it's a sunny summer evening you might prefer to indulge in outdoor drinks at the Pear Tree House (p155).

Getting There & Around

South Edinburgh covers a large area, and you'll need a bus to get to the farther-flung parts.

🚌 The main routes from the city centre are 10, 11, 15, 16, 23, 27 and 36 from Princes St to Tollcross, and 3, 5, 7, 8, 29, 31, 37, 47 and 49 from North Bridge to Newington.

Neighbourhood Map on p148

The Meadows (p150) KAY ROXBY/ALAMY ©

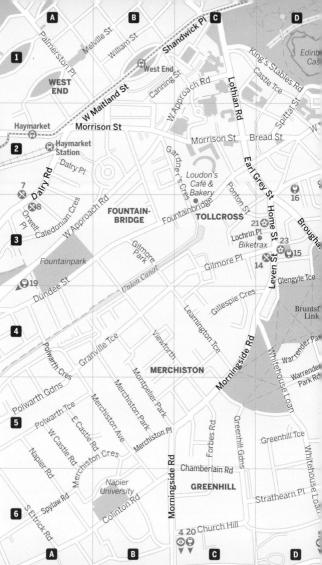

A B C D

1

Palmerston Pl
Melville St
William St
Shandwick Pl
West End
WEST
END
King's Stables Rd
Castle Tce
Edinb
Cas
W Maitland St
Canning St
W Approach Rd
Lothian Rd
Spittal St

2

Haymarket
Morrison St
Morrison St
Bread St
Haymarket
Station
Dalry Rd
Dalry Pl
7
8
Orwell
Pl
Caledonian Cres
W Approach Rd
Gardner's Cres
Loudon's
Café &
Bakery
Fountainbridge
Ponton St
Earl Grey St
Home St
16
TOLLCROSS
21
Brougha

3

FOUNTAIN-
BRIDGE
Fountainpark
Gilmore
Park
Gilmore Pl
Lochrin Pl
Biketrax
14
23
15
Leven St
Glengyle Tce
Bruntsf
Link

4

19
Dundee St
Union Canal
Gillespie Cres
Leamington Tce
Morningside Rd
Whitehouse L
Warrender Pa
Warrender
Park Rd

MERCHISTON

Granville Tce
Viewforth
Montpelier Park
Polwarth Cres

5

Polwarth Gdns
Polwarth Tce
E Castle Rd
Merchiston Ave
Merchiston Park
Merchiston Pl
Merchiston Cres
W Castle Rd
Forbes Rd
Greenhill Gdns
Greenhill Rd
Greenhill Tce
Whitehouse Loan
Napier Rd
Chamberlain Rd
GREENHILL

6

S Ettrick Rd
Spylaw Rd
Napier
University
Colinton Rd
Morningside Rd
Strathearn Pl
4 20 Church Hill

A B C D

E

High St
(Royal Mile)

F

OLD TOWN

G

H

Holyrood Rd

1

Cowgate

George IV Bridge

Chambers St

South Bridge

Edinburgh
University
Campus

nston Tce

Grassmarket

Greyfriars
Kirkyard

National Museum
of Scotland

Surgeons' Hall
Museums

The Pleasance

Viewcraig
Gdns

inburgh
llege
Art

Keir St

George
Heriot's
School

Teller Hall

9

22

Potterrow

1

Brown St

2

Lauriston Pl

Teviot Pl

Bristo
Sq

Edinburgh
University

10

24

Holyrood
Park

Chalmers St

Nightingale
Way

Simpson Loan

Quartermile

George Sq

13

W Nicolson
St

18

E Crosscauseway

Nicolson St

St Leonard's St

11

University
Library

Buccleuch Pl

25

12

17

Rankeillor St

3

Meadow La

Buccleuch St

LAURISTON

3

The Meadows

S Bernard Tce

6

Melville Dr

Summerhall

2

S Clerk St

26

E Preston St

4

Argyle Pl

Melville Tce

Sciennes

Newington Rd

Spottiswoode St

Arden St

Marchmont Rd

Roseneath
St

Sciennes Rd

Hatton Pl

Causewayside

Salisbury
Pl

5

Chalmers Cres

Grange Rd

Cumin Pl

Seton Pl

Findhorn Pl

Causewayside

Spottiswoode Rd

MARCHMONT

Thirlestane Rd

Beaufort Rd

Kilgraston Rd

Grange
Cemetery

Mansionhouse Rd

Lauder Rd

Strathearn Rd

Hope Tce

Dick Pl

Blackford Rd

For reviews see

⊙	Sights	p150
⊗	Eating	p151
⊖	Drinking	p154
✿	Entertainment	p156
⌂	Shopping	p157

N 0

0

500 m

0.25 miles

E

Grange Loan

F

G

H

South Edinburgh

Sights

Surgeons' Hall Museums

MUSEUM

1 MAP P148, G2

Housed in a grand Ionic temple designed by William Playfair in 1832, these three fascinating museums were originally established as teaching collections. The **History of Surgery Museum** provides a look at surgery in Scotland from the 15th century to the present day. Highlights include the exhibit on murderers Burke and Hare (p55), which includes Burke's death mask and a pocketbook made from his skin, and a display on Dr Joseph Bell, who was the inspiration for the character of Sherlock Holmes.

The adjacent **Dental Collection**, with its wince-inducing extraction tools, covers the history of dentistry, while the **Pathology Museum** houses a gruesome but compelling 19th-century collection of diseased organs and massive tumours pickled in formaldehyde. (☏0131-527 1711; www.museum.rcsed.ac.uk; Nicolson St; adult/child £7/4; ☉10am-5pm; ☐3, 5, 7, 8, 14, 30, 31, 33)

Summerhall

GALLERY

2 MAP P148, H4

The Summerhall cultural centre houses several permanent art displays, and stages changing exhibitions of contemporary art. (☏0131-560 1580; www.summerhall.co.uk; 1 Summerhall; admission free; ☉11am-6pm Tue-Sun; ☐41, 42, 67)

Gilmerton Cove

While ghost tours of Edinburgh's underground vaults and haunted graveyards have become a mainstream attraction, **Gilmerton Cove** (☏07914 829177; www.gilmertoncove.org.uk; 16 Drum St; adult/child £7.50/4; ☉tours 11am-3pm Mon-Fri, noon-3pm Sat & Sun Apr-Sep, noon Mon-Fri, noon & 2pm Sat & Sun Oct-Mar) remains an off-the-beaten-track gem. Hidden in the southern suburbs, the mysterious 'cove' is a series of subterranean caverns hacked out of the rock, their origin and function unknown. Advance bookings essential through **Rosslyn Tours** (☏07914 829177; www.rosslyntours.co.uk).

The Meadows

PARK

3 MAP P148, F3

This mile-long stretch of lush grass criss-crossed with tree-lined walks was once a shallow lake known as the Borough Loch. Drained in the 1740s and converted into parkland, it's a great place for a picnic or a quiet stroll – in springtime its walks lie ankle-deep in drifts of pink cherry blossom, and there are great views of Arthur's Seat. (Melville Dr; ☐all Tollcross, South Bridge buses)

Hermitage of Braid

WILDLIFE RESERVE

4 ◎ MAP P148, C6

The Hermitage of Braid is a wooded valley criss-crossed with walking trails to the south of Blackford Hill – with sunlight filtering through the leaves and the sound of birdsong all around, you'll feel miles from the city. **Hermitage House** (⏱9am-4pm Mon-Fri, noon-4pm Sun, closed Sat), an 18th-century mansion, houses a visitor centre that explains the history and wildlife of the glen, and has details of nearby nature trails. (www.fohb.org; ☐5, 11, 15, 16)

Blackford Hill

VIEWPOINT

5 ◎ MAP P148, D6

A patch of countryside enclosed by the city's southern suburbs, craggy Blackford Hill (164m) offers pleasant walking and splendid views. The panorama to the north takes in Edinburgh Castle atop its rock, the bristling spine of the Old Town, the monuments on Calton Hill and the 'sleeping lion' of Arthur's Seat. (Charterhall Rd; ☐24, 38, 41)

Eating

Aizle

SCOTTISH ££

6 ✕ MAP P148, H3

If you tend to have trouble deciding what to eat, Aizle (the name is an old Scots word for 'spark' or 'ember') will do the job for you. There's no menu here, just a five-course dinner conjured from a monthly 'harvest' of the finest and freshest local produce (listed on a blackboard), and presented beautifully – art on a plate. (☎0131-662 9349; http://aizle.co.uk; 107-109 St Leonard's St; 5-course dinner £55; ⏱5-9pm Wed-Sat; 🛜; ☐14)

Locanda de Gusti

ITALIAN ££

7 ✕ MAP P148, A3

This bustling family bistro, loud with the buzz of conversation and the clink of glasses and cutlery, is no ordinary Italian but a little corner of Naples, complete with hearty Neapolitan home cooking by friendly head chef Rosario. The food ranges from light and tasty ravioli tossed with butter and sage to delicious platters of grilled seafood. (☎0131-346 8800; www.locandadegusti.com; 102 Dalry Rd; mains £14-26; ⏱5.30-10pm Mon-Wed, 12.30-2pm & 5.30-10pm Thu-Sat; 👶; ☐2, 3, 4, 25, 33, 44)

First Coast

SCOTTISH ££

8 ✕ MAP P148, A3

This popular neighbourhood bistro has a striking main dining area with sea-blue wood panelling and stripped stonework, and a short and simple menu offering hearty comfort food such as fish with creamy mash, brown shrimp and garlic butter, or pigeon breast with black pudding, pearl barley and beetroot. Lunchtime and early evening there's an excellent two-course meal for £13.50. (☎0131-313 4404; www.first-coast.co.uk; 97-101

Brunch at Loudon's

One of South Edinburgh's favourite places to kick back over brunch with the weekend papers, **Loudon's** (Map p148, C3; www.loudons.co.uk; 94b Fountainbridge; mains £8-13; ⏰7.30am-5pm Mon-Fri, 8am-5pm Sat & Sun; 🛜🖊️👶; 🚌1, 34, 300) bakes its own organic bread on the premises, serves ethically sourced coffee, and has an all-day brunch menu (till 4pm) on Saturday and Sunday.

Dalry Rd; mains £13-20; ⏰noon-2pm & 5-11pm Mon-Sat; 🛜🖊️👶; 🚌2, 3, 4, 25, 33, 44)

Brew Lab
CAFE £

9 ⊗ MAP P148, G2

Students with iPads lolling in armchairs, sipping carefully crafted espressos amid artfully distressed brick and plaster, recycled school-gym flooring, old workshop benches and lab stools... this is coffee-nerd heaven. There's good food, too, with hearty soups and crusty baguette sandwiches. In summer, try the refreshing cold-brew coffee. (📞0131-662 8963; www.brewlabcoffee.co.uk; 6-8 S College St; mains £4-5; ⏰8am-6pm Mon, to 8pm Tue-Fri, 9am-8pm Sat & Sun; 🛜; 🚌all South Bridge buses)

Field Southside
SCOTTISH ££

10 ⊗ MAP P148, G2

A tiny restaurant punching way above its weight, Field pulls off that rare feat: fine dining at modest prices. The food is Scottish, contemporary, and beautifully plated, all eaten while overlooked by a giant cow painted on one wall. The lunch/pre-theatre menu of three courses for £16.95 (available noon to 2pm and 5.30pm to 6.45pm) is extraordinarily good value. (📞0131-667 7010; www.fieldrestaurant.co.uk; 41 W Nicolson St; mains £13-19; ⏰noon-2pm & 5.30-9pm Tue-Sat; 🚌41, 42, 67)

Söderberg (The Meadows)
CAFE £

11 ⊗ MAP P148, F3

This Swedish-style coffee house produces its own home-baked pastries and breads, which form the basis of lunchtime sandwiches with fillings such as roast beef with beetroot and caper salad, and roast butternut squash with sunblush tomato pesto. Breakfast (served till noon) can be a basket of breads with conserves and cheeses, or yoghurt with granola and fruit. (📞0131-228 5876; www.soderberg.uk; 27 Simpson Loan; mains £6-10; ⏰7.30am-7pm Mon-Fri, 9am-7pm Sat & Sun; 🖊️👶; 🚌23, 27, 45, 47, 300)

Kalpna

INDIAN £

12 🚫 MAP P148, H3

A long-standing Edinburgh favourite, Kalpna is one of the best Indian restaurants in the country, vegetarian or otherwise. The cuisine is mostly Gujarati, with a smattering of dishes from other parts of India. The all-you-can-eat lunch buffet (£8.50) is superb value. (📞0131-667 9890; www.kalpnarestaurant.com; 2-3 St Patrick Sq; mains £8-13; ⏰noon-2pm & 5.30-10.30pm; 🍴; 🚌all Newington buses)

Buffalo Grill

STEAK ££

13 🚫 MAP P148, G2

The Buffalo Grill is cramped, noisy, fun and always busy, so book ahead. An American-style menu offers burgers, steaks and side orders of fries and onion rings, along with fish and chicken dishes, shrimp tempura and a handful of vegetarian options, but the steaks are the main event. (📞0131-667 7427; www.buffalogrill.co.uk; 12-14 Chapel St; mains £11-25; ⏰11am-3pm & 5pm-late Mon-Thu, 11am-late Fri & Sat, 5pm-late Sun; 🚌41, 42, 67)

Tuk Tuk

INDIAN £

14 🚫 MAP P148, D3

One of Edinburgh's livelier Indian restaurants, Tuk Tuk serves street-food-style Indian dishes in spacious surroundings with vintage Bollywood posters on the wall. The menu boasts classics such as *channa puri* (curried chickpeas with flatbread) and an excellent signature 'railway station' curry (lamb on the bone, as served on

Loudon's

Indian railways). Popular with bigger groups and pre- and post-theatre crowds. (📞 0131-228 3322; www.tuktukonline.com; 1 Leven St; mains £5-6; ⏱ noon-10.30pm Sun-Thu, to 10.45pm Fri & Sat; 🚌 11, 15, 16, 23, 36, 45)

Drinking

Bennet's Bar   PUB

🔢 15 🍺 MAP P148, D3

Situated beside the King's Theatre (p157), Bennet's (established in 1839) has managed to hang on to almost all of its beautiful Victorian fittings, from the leaded stained-glass windows and the ornate mirrors to the wooden gantry and the brass water taps on the bar (for your whisky – there are over 100 malts from which to choose).

(📞 0131-229 5143; www.bennetsbar edinburgh.co.uk; 8 Leven St; ⏱ 11am-1am; 🚌 all Tollcross buses)

Royal Dick   MICROBREWERY

Located in Summerhall (see 2 ⊚ Map p148, H4), the decor at the Royal Dick alludes to its past as the home of Edinburgh University's veterinary school: there are shelves of laboratory glassware and walls covered with animal bones, even an old operating table. But rather than being creepy, it's a warm, welcoming place for a drink, serving artisan ales and craft gins produced by its own microbrewery and distillery. (📞 0131-560 1572; www.summerhall.co.uk/the-royal-dick; 1 Summerhall; ⏱ noon-1am Mon-Sat, 12.30pm-midnight Sun; 📶; 🚌 41, 42, 67)

Bennet's Bar

Brauhaus BAR

16 MAP P148, D2

This bar is fairly small – half a dozen bar stools, a couple of sofas and a scattering of seats – but its ambition is huge, with a vast menu of bottled beers from all over the world, ranging from the usual suspects (Belgium, Germany and the Czech Republic) to more unusual brews and more than 60 single-malt whiskies. (☏0131-447 7721; 105 Lauriston Pl; ⏰5pm-1am Sun-Fri, 3pm-1am Sat; ☜; ☒23, 27, 45, 47, 300)

Auld Hoose PUB

17 MAP P148, H3

Promoting itself as the South-side's only 'alternative' pub, the Auld Hoose certainly lives up to its reputation, with unpretentious decor, gig posters on the walls, a range of real ales from remote Scottish microbreweries, a regular quiz night (8pm Tuesday) and a jukebox that would make the late John Peel weep with joy. (☏0131-668 2934; www.theauldhoose.co.uk; 23-25 St Leonards St; ⏰noon-12.45am Mon-Sat, 12.30pm-12.45am Sun; ☜☺; ☒14)

Pear Tree House PUB

18 MAP P148, G2

Set in an 18th-century house with a cobbled courtyard, the Pear Tree is a student favourite with an open fire in winter, bright modern decor inside, and the city's biggest and most popular beer garden in summer. (☏0131-667 7533; www.

The Union Canal

Built 200 years ago and abandoned in the 1960s, the Union Canal was restored and reopened to navigation in 2002. Edinburgh Quays, its city-centre terminus in Tollcross, is a starting point for canal cruises, towpath walks and bike rides. The canal stretches west for 31 miles through the rural landscape of West Lothian to Falkirk, where it joins the Forth and Clyde Canal at the Falkirk Wheel boat lift. At Harrison Park, a mile southwest of Edinburgh Quays, is a pretty little canal basin with rowing boats for hire.

pear-tree-house.co.uk; 38 W Nicolson St; ⏰11am-1am; ☜; ☒2, 41, 42, 47)

Caley Sample Room PUB

19 MAP P148, A3

The Sample Room is a big, lively, convivial pub serving a wide range of wines and excellent real ales, and some of the best pub grub in the city (brunch served 10am to 4pm at weekends). It's popular with sports fans, too, who gather to watch football and rugby matches on the large-screen TVs. (☏0131-337 7204; www.thecaley sampleroom.co.uk; 58 Angle Park Tce; ⏰noon-midnight Mon-Thu, to 1am Fri, 10am-1am Sat, 10am-midnight Sun; ☜☺; ☒4, 28, 34, 44, 300)

Canny Man's PUB

20 MAP P148, C6

A lovely eccentric pub, the Canny Man's consists of a crowded warren of tiny rooms crammed with a bizarre collection of antiques and curiosities (a description that could apply to some of the regulars). If you can get in, you'll find it serves excellent real ale, vintage port and Cuban cigars, and the best Bloody Marys in town. (☏0131-447 1484; www.cannymans.co.uk; 237 Morningside Rd; 📶; 🚌11, 15, 16, 17, 23)

Entertainment

Summerhall THEATRE

Formerly Edinburgh University's veterinary school, the Summerhall complex (see 2 ⊙ Map p148, H4) is a major cultural centre and entertainment venue, with old halls and lecture theatres (including an original anatomy lecture theatre) now serving as venues for drama, dance, cinema and comedy performances. It's also one of the main venues for **Edinburgh Festival** (☏0131-473 2000; www.eif.co.uk; ⊙Aug) events. (☏0131-560 1580; www.summerhall.co.uk; 1 Summerhall; ⊙box office 10am-6pm; 🚌41, 42, 67)

Entrance to the King's Theatre

Cameo

CINEMA

1 ⭐ MAP P148, D3

The three-screen, independently
owned Cameo is a good old-
fashioned cinema showing an
imaginative mix of mainstream
and art-house movies. There's a
good program of late-night films
and Sunday matinees, and the
seats in screen 1 are big enough
to get lost in. (☎0871 902 5723;
www.picturehouses.com/cinema/
Cameo_Picturehouse; 38 Home St; ☎;
☐all Tollcross buses)

Edinburgh Festival Theatre

THEATRE

22 ⭐ MAP P148, G2

A beautifully restored art-deco
theatre with a modern all-glass
frontage, the Festival is the city's
main venue for opera, dance and
ballet, but also stages musicals,
concerts, drama and children's
shows. (☎0131-529 6000; www.
capitaltheatres.com/festival;
13-29 Nicolson St; ⏰box office 10am-
7.30pm; ☐all South Bridge buses)

King's Theatre

THEATRE

23 ⭐ MAP P148, D3

The King's is a traditional theatre
with a program of musicals,
drama, comedy and its famous
Christmas pantomimes. (☎0131-
529 6000; www.capitaltheatres.com/
kings; 2 Leven St; ⏰box office 10am-
6pm; ☐all Tollcross buses)

Shopping

Lighthouse

BOOKS

24 🔒 MAP P148, G2

Lighthouse is a radical independent bookshop that supports both
small publishers and local writers.
It stocks a wide range of political, gay and feminist literature, as
well as non-mainstream fiction
and nonfiction. (☎0131-662 9112;
http://lighthousebookshop.com; 43 W
Nicolson St; ⏰10am-6pm Mon-Sat,
11.30am-5pm Sun; ☐41, 42, 67)

Backbeat

MUSIC

25 🔒 MAP P148, H3

If you're hunting for second-hand
vinyl from way back, this cramped
little shop has a stunning and con-
stantly changing collection of jazz,
blues, rock and soul, plus lots of
'60s and '70s stuff, though you'll
have to take some time to hunt
through the clutter. (☎0131-668
2666; 31 E Crosscauseway; ⏰10am-
5.30pm Mon-Sat; ☐all Newington
buses)

Meadows Pottery

CERAMICS

26 🔒 MAP P148, H4

This little shop sells a range of
colourful, high-fired oxidised
stoneware, both domestic and
decorative, all hand thrown on the
premises. If you can't find what
you want, you can commission
custom-made pieces. (☎0131-662
4064; www.themeadowspottery.com;
11a Summerhall Pl; ⏰10am-6pm Mon-
Fri, to 5pm Sat; ☐2, 41, 42, 67)

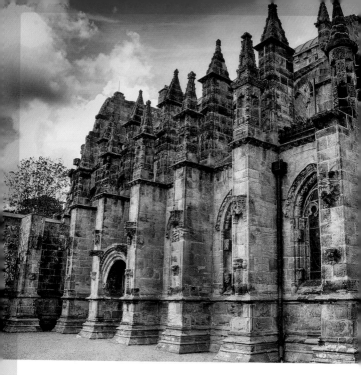

Worth a Trip 🔭
Rosslyn Chapel

Many years may have passed since Dan Brown's novel The Da Vinci Code *and the subsequent film came out, but floods of visitors still descend on Scotland's most beautiful and enigmatic church – Rosslyn Chapel. Built in the mid-15th century for Sir William St Clair, third prince of Orkney, its ornately carved interior is a monument to the mason's art.*

Collegiate Church of St Matthew

www.rosslynchapel.com

Chapel Loan, Roslin

adult/child £9/free

🕒 9.30am-6pm Mon-Sat Jun-Aug, to 5pm Sep-May, noon-4.45pm Sun year-round

The Apprentice Pillar

Perhaps the most beautiful carving in the chapel, the Apprentice Pillar is at the entrance to the Lady Chapel. Four vines spiral around the pillar, issuing from the mouths of eight dragons at its base. At the top is an image of Isaac, son of Abraham, upon the altar.

Lucifer, the Fallen Angel

At head height in the Lady Chapel, to the left of the second window from the left, is an upside-down angel bound with rope, a symbol often associated with freemasonry. The arch above is decorated with the Dance of Death.

The Green Man

On the boss at the base of the arch between the second and third windows from the left in the Lady Chapel is the Green Man. It's the finest example of more than 100 carvings of the Green Man, a pagan symbol of spring, fertility and rebirth.

Indian Corn?

The frieze around the second window in the south wall is said to represent Indian corn (maize), but it predates Columbus' discovery of the New World in 1492.

The Apprentice

High in the southwestern corner, beneath an empty statue niche, is the head of the murdered apprentice; there's a deep wound in his forehead, above the right eye. According to legend, the stonemason's apprentice created a pillar (the Apprentice Pillar) more exquisitely carved than anything the mason himself could achieve, and, in a fit of jealousy, the mason murdered his apprentice.

The Ceiling

The spectacular ceiling vault is decorated with engraved roses, lilies and stars; can you spot the sun and the moon?

★ **Top Tips**

○ No photography or video is allowed inside the chapel.

○ It's worth buying the official guidebook by the Earl of Rosslyn (£5), finding a bench in the gardens and having a skim through before going into the chapel – the background informa-tion will make your visit all the more interesting.

✕ **Take a Break**

There's a **coffee shop** (Chapel Loan, Roslin; mains £4-9; ◷ 9.30am-6pm Mon-Sat Jun-Aug, to 5pm Sep-May, noon-4.45pm Sun year-round; ▣ 37) in the chapel's visi-tor centre, serving soup, sandwiches, coffee and cake, with a view over Roslin Glen.

★ **Getting There**

Lothian Bus 37 to Penicuik Deanburn links Edinburgh to the village of Roslin. (Bus 37 to Bush does not go via Roslin.)

Survival Guide

Grassmarket (p47), Old Town KUMAR SRISKANDAN/ALAMY ©

Before You Go

Book Your Stay

○ Hotels and hostels are found throughout the Old and New Towns; midrange B&Bs and guesthouses are concentrated outside the centre in the suburbs of Tollcross, Bruntsfield, Newington and Pilrig.

○ If you're driving, don't even think about staying in the city centre unless your hotel has its own private car park – parking in the centre is a nightmare.

○ Edinburgh is packed to the gills during the festival period (August) and over Hogmanay (New Year). If you want a room during these periods, book as far in advance as you can – a year ahead if possible.

○ It's best to book at least a few months ahead for accommodation at Easter and from mid-May to mid-September.

○ Edinburgh accommodation costs: budget is less than £65, midrange

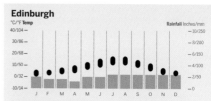

Edinburgh

When to Go

○ **Winter** (Dec–Feb) Cold and dark, occasional snow; Christmas decorations, Hogmanay and Burns Night celebrations.

○ **Spring** (Mar–May) Cold to mild, damp, occasional sun; flowers and blossom everywhere.

○ **Summer** (Jun–Aug) Mild to warm but occasionally wet; main tourist season, city packed out for festival in August.

○ **Autumn** (Sep–Nov) Mild to chilly, often damp; autumn colours in parks, tourist crowds have left.

is £65 to £130, and top end is more than £130, based on the cost of a double room with breakfast.

○ If you're staying for a week or more, a short-term or serviced apartment might be more economical.

○ If you arrive in Edinburgh without a place to stay, the **Edinburgh tourist office** (Edinburgh iCentre; Map p50; ☎0131-473 3868; www. visitscotland.com/info/ services/edinburgh-icentre-p234441; Waverley Mall, 3 Princes St; ⊙9am-7pm Mon-Sat, 10am-7pm Sun Jul

& Aug, to 6pm Jun, to 5pm Sep-May; 🛜; 🚇St Andrew Sq) booking service will try to find a room to suit you (and will charge a £5 fee if successful). If you have the time, pick up the tourist office's accommodation brochure and ring around yourself.

Useful Websites

VisitScotland (www. visitscotland.com/ edinburgh) Wide range of options from the official website.

Lonely Planet (www. lonelyplanet.com/ hotels) Recommendations and bookings.

This Is Edinburgh
(www.edinburgh.org)
Promotional website
with wide range of
accommodation and
weekend-break offers.

Best Budget

Code Pod Hostel
(www.codehostel.com)
Stylish, modern hostel
in a cobbled New Town
backstreet.

**Edinburgh Central
SYHA** (www.syha.
org.uk) Hostelling
Scotland's five-star
establishment close to
the city centre.

Safestay Edinburgh
(www.safestay.com)
A big, bright, modern
hostel in the heart of
the Old Town.

Best Midrange

Sheridan Guest House
(www.sheridan
edinburgh.com) A little
haven hidden away to
the north of the New
Town.

Two Hillside Crescent
(www.twohillside
crescent.com) A
gorgeous Georgian
overlooking peaceful
gardens.

14 Hart Street
(http://14hartstreet.
co.uk) Elegant quarters
nestled close to the
bars and restaurants of
Broughton St.

Best Top End

Pilrig House (www.pil-
righouse.com) Luxury
apartments in a historic
house overlooking a
peaceful park.

**Southside Guest
House** (www.southside
guesthouse.co.uk)
South Edinburgh town-
house that feels more
like a modern boutique
hotel.

**Witchery by the
Castle** (www.the
witchery.com) Nine lav-
ish Gothic suites in the
shadow of Edinburgh
Castle.

Arriving in Edinburgh

Edinburgh Airport

Edinburgh Airport
(EDI; ☎ 0844 448 8833;
www.edinburghairport.

com) Bus 100 runs
from the airport to
Waverley Bridge (one
way/return £4.50/7.50,
30 minutes), outside
the main train station,
via Haymarket and
the West End every 10
minutes from 4.30am
to 12.30am, and then
every 15 minutes until
4.15am. Trams run from
the airport to the city
centre (one way/return
£6/8.50, 33 minutes,
every six to eight
minutes from 6am to
midnight). An airport
taxi to the city centre
costs around £20 and
takes about 20 to 30
minutes.

Edinburgh Waverley Train Station

The main train station
is Edinburgh Waverley,
located in the heart of
the city between the
Old Town and New
Town. Trains arriving
from, and departing for,
the west also stop at
Edinburgh Haymarket
station, which is more
convenient for the West
End.

Getting Around

Bus

o Bus timetables, route maps and fare guides are posted at all main bus and tram stops, and you can pick up a copy of the free *Lothian Buses Route Map* from Lothian Buses Travelshops on **Waverley Bridge** (31 Waverley Bridge; ⊙9am-6pm Tue, Wed & Fri, to 7pm Mon & Thu, to 5.30pm Sat, 10am-5.30pm Sun; 🚌6) and **Hanover St** (27 Hanover St; ⊙9am-6pm Mon-Fri, to 5.30pm Sat; 🚌23, 27).

o Adult fares within the city are £1.70; purchase from the bus driver. Children aged under five travel free and those aged five to 15 pay a flat fare of 80p.

o On Lothian Buses you must pay the driver the exact fare, but First buses will give change. Lothian Bus drivers also sell a day ticket (£4) that gives unlimited travel on Lothian buses and trams for a day; a family day ticket (up to two adults and three children) costs £8.50.

o Night-service buses, which run hourly between midnight and 5am, charge a flat fare of £3.50.

o You can also buy a Ridacard (from Travel shops; not available from bus drivers) that gives unlimited travel for one week for £19.

o The Lothian Buses lost-property office is in the Hanover St Travelshop.

Tram

o Edinburgh's tram system (www. edinburghtrams.com) consists of one line from Edinburgh Airport to York Pl, at the top of Leith Walk, via Haymarket, the West End and Princes St.

o Tickets are integrated with the city's Lothian Buses, costing £1.70 for a single journey within the city boundary, or £6 to the airport.

o Trams run every eight to 10 minutes Monday to Saturday and every 12 to 15 minutes on Sunday, from 5.30am to 11pm.

Taxi

o Edinburgh's black taxis can be hailed in the street, ordered by phone (extra 80p charge) or picked up at one of the many central ranks.

o The minimum charge is £2.10 (£3.10 at night) for the first 450m, then 25p for every subsequent 184m – a typical 2-mile trip across the city centre will cost around £6 to £7.

o Tipping is up to you – because of the high fares, local people rarely tip on short journeys, but they occasionally

Bus Info On Your Phone

Transport for Edinburgh has created free smartphone apps that provide route maps, timetables and live waiting times for city buses and trams. Search for Transport for Edinburgh on the App Store (iOS) or Google Play (Android). The companion m-tickets app allows you to buy bus and tram tickets on your phone.

round up to the nearest 50p on longer ones.

Central Taxis (☎ 0131-229 2468; www.taxis-edinburgh.co.uk)

City Cabs (☎ 0131-228 1211; www.citycabs.co.uk)

ComCab (☎ 0131-272 8001; www.comcab-edinburgh.co.uk)

Bike

○ Edinburgh is well equipped with bike lanes and dedicated cycle tracks.

○ You can buy a map of the city's cycle routes from most bike shops.

○ **Biketrax** (Map p148, D3; ☎0131-228 6633; www.biketrax.co.uk; 11-13 Lochrin Pl; per day from £20; ⊙9.30am-6pm Mon-Fri, to 5.30pm Sat, noon-5pm Sun, longer hours Apr-Sep; 🚌all Tollcross buses) rents out mountain, hybrid, road, Brompton folding and electric bikes. You'll need a debit- or credit-card deposit and photographic ID.

Car & Motorcycle

○ Though useful for day trips beyond the city, a car in central Edinburgh is more of a liability than a convenience.

○ There's no parking on main roads into the city from 7.30am to 6.30pm Monday to Saturday. Also, parking in the city centre can be a nightmare.

○ On-street parking is controlled by self-service ticket machines from 8.30am to 6.30pm Monday to Saturday, and costs from £2.20 to £4.20 per hour, with a 30-minute to four-hour maximum.

○ All the big international car-rental agencies have offices in Edinburgh, including **Avis** (☎0844 544 6059; www.avis.co.uk; 24 E London St; ⊙8am-6pm Mon-Fri, to 3pm Sat, 10am-2pm Sun; 🚌8, 13, 27) and **Europcar** (☎0871 384 3453; www.europcar.co.uk; Platform 2, Waverley station; ⊙7am-5pm; 🚌all Princes St buses).

Emergency & Useful Phone Numbers

UK's country code	☎44
International access code	☎00
Police (emergency)	☎999
Police (non-emergency)	☎101
Fire	☎999
Ambulance	☎999

Essential Information

Accessible Travel

○ Download Lonely Planet's free Accessible Travel guide from http://lptravel.to/Accessible Travel.

○ Edinburgh's Old Town, with its steep hills, narrow closes, flights of stairs and cobbled streets, is a challenge for wheelchair users.

○ Large new hotels and modern tourist attractions are usually accessible; however, many B&Bs and guesthouses are in hard-to-adapt older buildings that lack ramps and lifts.

○ Newer buses have steps or kneeling

suspension that lowers for access, but it's wise to check before setting out. Most black taxis are wheelchair-friendly.

○ Many banks are fitted with induction loops to assist the hearing impaired. Some attractions have Braille guides for the visually impaired.

○ **VisitScotland** (www.visitscotland.com) has an online guide to accessible accommodation for travellers with disabilities.

Business Hours

Banks 9.30am to 4pm Monday to Friday; some branches open 9.30am to 1pm Saturday.

Businesses 9am to 5pm Monday to Friday.

Pubs and bars 11am to 11pm Monday to Thursday, to 1am Friday and Saturday, 12.30pm to 11pm Sunday.

Restaurants noon to 2.30pm and 6pm to 10pm.

Shops 9am to 5.30pm Monday to Saturday, some to 8pm Thursday; 11am to 5pm Sunday.

Discount Cards

○ If you plan to visit the Royal Yacht *Britannia*

as well as Edinburgh Castle and the Palace of Holyroodhouse, consider buying a **Royal Edinburgh Ticket** (https://edinburghtour.com/royal-edinburgh-ticket), which includes admission to all three plus unlimited travel on hop-on, hop-off tour buses among the various attractions.

Electricity

Type G
230V/50Hz

Money

ATMs

○ Automatic teller machines (ATMs – often called cashpoints) are widespread.

○ You can use Visa, MasterCard, Amex, Cirrus, Plus and Maestro cards to withdraw cash from ATMs belonging to most banks and building societies.

○ Cash withdrawals from non-bank ATMs, usually found in shops, may be subject to a charge of £1.50 or £2.

Currency

○ The unit of currency in the UK is the pound sterling (£).

○ One pound sterling consists of 100 pence (called 'p' colloquially).

○ Banknotes come in denominations of £5, £10, £20 and £50.

○ Scottish banks issue their own banknotes, meaning there's quite a variety of different notes in circulation. They are harder to exchange outside the UK, so swap for Bank of England notes before you leave.

Moneychanging

○ The best-value places to change money are post offices, where no commission is charged.

○ Be careful using bureaux de change; they may offer good exchange rates but frequently levy outrageous commissions and fees.

Tipping

Hotels One pound per bag is standard; gratuities for cleaning staff are completely at your discretion.

Pubs Tips are not expected unless table service is provided, then tip £1 for a round of drinks.

Restaurants For decent service tip 10% and up to 15% at more expensive places. Check to see if service has been added to the bill already (most likely for large groups).

Taxis Round fares up to the nearest pound.

Public Holidays

New Year's Day 1 January

New Year Bank Holiday 2 January

Spring Bank Holiday second Monday in April

Good Friday Friday before Easter Sunday

Easter Monday Monday following Easter Sunday

May Day first Monday in May

Phone Codes & Rates

International access code	☎ 00
Edinburgh area code	☎ 0131
Mobile phone numbers	☎ 07xxx; 10p to 20p per minute from landlines, 3p to 55p per minute from mobiles
Local calls	☎ 0845; up to 7p per minute from landlines & mobiles, plus access charge
National calls	☎ 0870; up to 13p per minute from landlines & mobiles, plus access charge
Premium calls	☎ 09; up to £3.60 per minute from landlines & mobiles, plus access charge, plus 5p to £6 per call
Toll-free numbers	☎ 0800 or 0808; free from UK landlines & mobiles

Christmas Day 25 December

Boxing Day 26 December

Safe Travel

○ Lothian Rd, Dalry Rd, Rose St and the western end of Princes St, at the junction with Shandwick Pl and Queensferry St, can get a bit rowdy late on Friday and Saturday nights after pub-closing time.

○ Calton Hill offers good views during the day but is best avoided at night.

○ Be aware that the area between Salamander St and Leith Links in Leith is a red-light district – lone women here at any time of day might be approached by kerb crawlers.

Telephones

○ There are plenty of public phones in Edinburgh, operated by coins, phonecards or credit cards; phonecards are available in newsagents.

○ Edinburgh's area code is 0131, followed by a seven-digit number. You only need to dial the 0131 prefix when you are calling Edinburgh from outside the city, or if you're dialling from a mobile.

○ To call overseas from the UK, dial the international access code (🖉00), then the area code (dropping any initial 🖉0), followed by the telephone number.

Mobile Phones

○ The UK uses the GSM 900/1800 network, which is compatible with the rest of Europe, Australia and New Zealand, but not with the North American GSM 1900 system or Japanese mobile technology.

○ If in doubt, check with your service provider; some North Americans have GSM 1900/900 phones that will work in the UK.

○ Edinburgh has excellent 4G coverage.

Toilets

○ Public toilets are mostly free to use and are spread across the city.

○ Most are open from 9am to 4pm, up to 8pm in summer.

○ Find the nearest one at www.edinburgh.gov.uk; search for 'public toilet'.

Tourist Information

Edinburgh Tourist Office (Edinburgh iCentre; Map p50, D2; 🖉 0131-473 3868; www.visitscotland.com/info/services/edinburgh-icentre-p234441; Waverley Mall, 3 Princes St; ⏱9am-7pm Mon-Sat, 10am-7pm Sun Jul & Aug, to 6pm Jun, to 5pm Sep-May; 🛜; 🚆St Andrew Sq) Accommodation booking service, currency exchange, gift shop and bookshop, internet access, and counters selling tickets for Edinburgh city tours and Scottish Citylink bus services.

Edinburgh Airport Tourist Office (🖉 0131-473 3690; www.visitscotland.com; East Terminal, Edinburgh Airport; ⏱7.30am-7.30pm Mon-Fri, to 7pm Sat & Sun) Visit Scotland Information Centre in the airport's terminal extension.

Visas

○ If you're a citizen of the EEA (European Economic Area) nations or Switzerland, you don't need a visa to enter or work in Britain – you can enter using your national identity card.

○ Visa regulations are always subject to change, which is especially likely after Britain's exit from the EU on 29 March 2019, so it's essential to check before leaving home.

○ Currently, if you're a citizen of Australia, Canada, New Zealand, Japan, Israel, the US and several other countries, you can stay for up to six months (no visa required) but are not allowed to work.

○ Nationals of many countries, including South Africa, will need to obtain a visa: for more info, see www.gov.uk/browse/visas-immigration.

Index

See also separate subindexes for:

⊗ **Eating p171**

⊜ **Drinking p172**

⊛ **Entertainment p173**

⊝ **Shopping p173**

Behind the Scenes

Send Us Your Feedback

We love to hear from travellers – your comments help make our books better. We read every word, and we guarantee that your feedback goes straight to the authors. Visit **lonelyplanet.com/contact** to submit your updates and suggestions.

Note: We may edit, reproduce and incorporate your comments in Lonely Planet products such as guidebooks, websites and digital products, so let us know if you don't want your comments reproduced or your name acknowledged. For a copy of our privacy policy visit lonelyplanet.com/privacy.

Neil's Thanks

Thanks to the friendly and helpful tourist office staff all over Scotland; to Steven Fallon, Keith Jeffrey, Fiona Garven, Derek McCrindle, Brendan Bolland, Jenny Neil, Tom and Christine Duffin, Steve Hall, Elaine Simpson, Peter Fallon and Duncan Pepper; and, as ever, to Carol Downie. Thanks also to James Smart and the whole editorial team at Lonely Planet.

Acknowledgements

Cover photograph: Royal Mile, Richard Taylor/4Corners ©

Photographs pp30-1 (from left): Lou armor; Koah; Jeff Whyte/ Shutterstock ©

This Book

This 5th edition of Lonely Planet's *Pocket Edinburgh* guidebook was curated, researched and written by Neil Wilson, with contributions by Sophie McGrath. Neil also wrote the previous edition. This guidebook was produced by the following:

Destination Editor Clifton Wilkinson

Senior Product Editor Genna Patterson

Product Editor Jenna Myers

Senior Cartographer Mark Griffiths

Book Designer Clara Monitto

Assisting Editors Sarah Bailey, Victoria Harrison, Sarah Stewart

Cover Researcher Naomi Parker

Thanks to Olivia Devine, Bruce Evans, Jan Hankin, Martine Power

Our Writers

Neil Wilson

Neil was born in Scotland and has lived there most of his life. Based in Perthshire, he has been a full-time writer since 1988, working on more than 80 guidebooks for various publishers, including the Lonely Planet guides to Scotland, England, Ireland and Prague. An outdoors enthusiast since childhood, Neil is an active hill-walker, mountain-biker, sailor, snowboarder, fly-fisher and rock-climber, and has climbed and tramped in four continents, including ascents of Jebel Toubkal in Morocco, Mount Kinabalu in Borneo, the Old Man of Hoy in Scotland's Orkney Islands and the Northwest Face of Half Dome in California's Yosemite Valley.

Contributing writer: Sophie McGrath

Published by Lonely Planet Global Limited
CRN 554153
5th edition – Apr 2019
ISBN 978 1 78657 802 0
© Lonely Planet 2019   Photographs © as indicated 2019
10 9 8 7 6 5 4 3 2 1
Printed in Malaysia

Although the authors and Lonely Planet have taken all reasonable care in preparing this book, we make no warranty about the accuracy or completeness of its content and, to the maximum extent permitted, disclaim all liability arising from its use.

All rights reserved. No part of this publication may be copied, stored in a retrieval system, or transmitted in any form by any means, electronic, mechanical, recording or otherwise, except brief extracts for the purpose of review, and no part of this publication may be sold or hired, without the written permission of the publisher. Lonely Planet and the Lonely Planet logo are trademarks of Lonely Planet and are registered in the US Patent and Trademark Office and in other countries. Lonely Planet does not allow its name or logo to be appropriated by commercial establishments, such as retailers, restaurants or hotels. Please let us know of any misuses: lonelyplanet.com/ip.